DESTINATION:
Soulmate

A modern day
road map to
Happily Ever After
and manifesting
the love of your life
in as little as
eight weeks!

EMYRALD SINCLAIRE

This book is dedicated to all the single women out there who still have hope and faith that Prince Charming exists. This book is your guide. Keep the faith, *he* is on his way.

Table of Contents

S top me if you know this one...
Once upon a time, there was a beautiful young lady. But this was no ordinary lady! She was a Princess…only she didn't know it.

And so she spent her days in solitude forced to sweep and clean and do the bidding of her evil adopted family. They also didn't know who she was and they were horrible to the little girl.

They always told her she would never amount to anything, and anytime she was naive enough to share a wish or hope or dream, they would CRUSH it while laughing at her and telling her she was too stupid and just a peasant girl, after all.

As you can see, life was very rough on this girl and yet…she still kept the dream alive in her heart that one day Prince Charming would come and save her from her humble beginnings and that wretched family.

Doesn't that sound familiar?

Is it not the beginning of practically every single fairy tale about love you've ever heard as a little girl?

It's the 'hero's journey,' and it's entrenched deep into our blood.

But the reason it resonates with your heart and soul, dear one, is because your feminine heart yearns for a love that can transcend all barriers.

Your heart desires a magical Happily Ever After filled with True Love and a man who would slay dragons for you! A man who can make everything all better by merely riding up on a white horse and whisking you away to some magical far off land.

So where is this Prince Charming, you ask?

Does he really even exist?

I don't know about you, but when I was a child, I believed in magic. And no, not Harry Potter and Lord of the Rings type of magic.

But magic spells and transformation in the blink of an eye from servant to Princess type of magic!

And as I got older, the magic started to fade. If you're like me, you've been hurt too many times to count. You got confused and gave your heart away too many times to the wrong men. Looking around, you only saw couples who argued and were bitter and poked at each other. You saw nagging wives and unfaithful husbands.

And so the dream of Happily Ever After started to fade.

Maybe my Prince is NOT coming, you thought...

And even worse...maybe a fairy tale is only something you tell little girls to get them to fall asleep.

And if you became cynical, you also became angry at the whole concept of fairy tales. *They've been lying to us! I'm going to tell my daughter the real story,* you exclaimed!

Well, honey, there is no such thing as Prince Charming. One day you'll meet a man that you like very much. You'll give your heart and soul away to him. You'll think he's going to change everything for you. But eventually, that will change. You'll settle into a routine. You'll fight and bicker and start to blame each other for everything. You'll think it's his fault you lost your perfect body after having kids. You'll stop sleeping together as much. He'll eventually have an affair with his 22-year-old secretary. You'll take up tennis lessons and flirt with your instructor. But you know, that's life. And it's good enough. And as long as he is filthy rich, you won't mind too much, sweetie. Just make sure you find one with money and everything will be ok.

Isn't THAT some version of the truth nowadays?

So how do we shatter THAT mirror of reality and create your own real-life fairy tale?

And that, my dear, is precisely what this book is all about. Letting go of what you see around you and using the inspiration of all the stories we grew up with as children as a guide towards your own Happily Ever After.

Which I assure you, is entirely possible.

You just have to BELIEVE that it is possible.

If Fiona didn't honestly believe her prince would come, do you think she would have waited in the tower of a castle with a dragon guarding her for so long? No way! That feisty lady would have gone off and been the Queen of her own Queendom!

If Cinderella didn't honestly believe in her heart that love would win her Prince over, do you think she would have gone to the ball!? Not a chance. She would have stayed home singing to the mice and mopping the floors.

And how about Snow White? If I recall correctly, she spent her days frolicking through the forest singing about the fact that 'one day my Prince will come...'

These women were onto something!

You have to BELIEVE in your heart without a doubt that your Prince will come....

Because if you do not believe that something will happen, you will not take action towards achieving that desire.

If you stay stuck in the mentality that 'there are no good men in my town' or 'I'm too old/fat/skinny/dumb to be with someone good,' then you will not take action towards achieving true love.

You see where I'm going here, beauty?

We are going to grow your FAITH muscle by 1000%. And as a result, I promise you, true love shall find thee.

Follow your fairy godmother (that's ME, by the way), and I'll show you the way to your heart's desire!

SO HOW DOES THIS ALL WORK?

Let me first ask you a question, sweetheart.

If you went to the gym and hired a personal trainer to get fit, would you expect your personal trainer to do the push-ups for you? Would you expect him/her to actually do all of the exercises on the machine while you watched? And, then when he was done, you went home and thought to yourself, "Boy! I sure am getting stronger; I can feel it!"

Of course, you wouldn't.

Because just watching him do the exercises is NOT enough to help YOU become stronger.

It's the EXACT same thing here.

You can READ my book, but that will NOT cause much change in your life.

The ONLY way you can expect your life to change radically will be if you actually DO every single exercise that I outline in this book. And promise me, you will NOT move forward in the book until you complete the previous exercise. Yes, you can read a book and LEARN new information. But it's the PRACTICAL APPLICATION that is going to create lasting change in your life.

For example: How did you begin walking? Did you simply read a book on walking and 'think' about how to walk correctly and then lo and behold... you were walking?

No!

You crawled first. Then you stood up. You wobbly placed one foot in front of the other. And then...you fell down. But you continued to practice. You got back up and put one foot in front of the other, time and time again.

This book is the same. If you want Prince Charming, you have to be ready to get up and to fall down. Things will get messy. But if you continue to press onward, I promise you, you will be AMAZED at how your life transforms in such a short amount of time!

You're going to have to exercise your trust muscle and put your faith in a stranger who loves you very much (me!). I've put this book together in a particular way (after working with countless clients and guiding many, many women through my online course on Love Attraction called "Attract the One" - (www.emyraldsinclaire.com/attract). If you're curious as to how to take the exercises in this book and go deeper, there is a specific process that I've seen work with my clients, and it's going to work for you!

If...

You actually DO the exercises, meditations, and work that I outline here.

And so, I'm going to ask you to do two things before we even begin.

1. Make space in your life for the journey we are going to take together. Commit 30 minutes in your schedule every single day until you're done with this book. The exercises build on each other, and the momentum will build! You'll raise your vibration and continue to build excitement that Prince Charming IS on his way. And YES, you do deserve him, and you'd better get excited, girl! Because this is it!

2. Visit this website: www.emyraldsinclaire.com/destinationsoulmate and make sure to put in your name and email address so that you can download all the free resources designed to go along with this book

DISCLAIMERS:

1. While I primarily speak on heterosexual relationships and this book is geared towards heterosexual women, trust me, this works for everyone regardless of your age, location, weight, sexual preferences, shoe size, or whatever. The work is an inside job. It doesn't matter if you're gay, straight, bisexual, or

some other definition of your sexual orientation, if you do the work, your love life will change for the better! Promise.

2. You might have done some of these exercises before. Do them again. You're at a different place in your life, and there is an excellent chance you'll have a different awareness this time than the FIRST time you did the work. Some of the exercises might be new. Some might seem strange. Some might even make you think, *dang, this girl cray-cray.* But if you can put judgments aside and remind yourself that THESE EXACT EXERCISES are the ones that have helped my clients to achieve the end goal of 'meeting the one,' then I think you'll be okay. In fact, I KNOW you'll be more than okay. You'll be in love with yourself, in love with your life and ecstatic because guess who has shown up in your life?!

The One.

HERE'S WHAT YOU NEED IN ADDITION TO THIS BOOK:

1. A specific journal to be used for these exercises only. We are going on a journey. I'm giving you the road map. And think of your journal as the observations along the way of a most excellent adventure! Also, make sure to download the free resources that are meant to go along with this book. www.emyraldsinclaire.com/destinationsoulmate

2. An open mind. Remember above how I said we are going to be going through a bunch of new stuff here? Be open to change regardless of what you've experienced in your past. If you're reading this, it's because you're not where you want to be. Which means what you've been doing has NOT been working. So... by trying something new, you're going to get something different!

3. An open heart. I know you've probably been hurt in the past. How do I know this? You are human! We've all been hurt. But honestly, the most important thing I could stress (even if you shut the book after reading this sentence) is that if you're looking for your soulmate you need to continue to EXPAND the love in your heart in any given moment. Once you close the door to your heart and succumb to the fears of your ego, such as "I'll never meet the one. There are no good men in my town," then stick a fork in ya, honey, because you are already done, my dear.

Ready? Let's manifest love!

How To Use This Book

This book is meant to help you manifest love. And manifesting love is an *inside job*. This book is filled with exercises and self-love practices designed to help you truly accept and love who you are! So whether you are single and looking for love, or already in a relationship, trust that *this book* will improve all of your relationships, because every relationship you have starts with the relationship you have with yourself.

There will be a lesson a day for 8 weeks. And I've designed it as a compliment to my online course, Attract the One. (www.emyraldsinclaire.com/attract) But you don't have to enroll in the course to get the benefits from this book. It's strong enough on its own to show you the path to love!

I suggest you pick a start date (today!) when you can dedicate about 30 minutes a day (every day) for the next 8 weeks. Yes, it's okay if you miss a day. Yes, it's okay if you want to stick with a particular lesson for longer than a day. But what I'm asking you to do is this: make a commitment to yourself to finish what you started.

And that's it.

Oh yeah, give yourself a pat on the back and a kiss on the shoulder. You deserve it. You deserve it all.

Xo,

Emyrald

Week 1

THE JOURNEY BEGINS!

"The journey of a thousand miles begins with a single step."

—Lao Tzu

Congrats! You've begun. You've made the critical decision to change your life. And I expect HUGE transformation within you over the next two months!

How do I know this?

Because I've seen it for countless clients.

Get this - did you know that only 17% of people finish a book they start to read? Yikes! And in 2018, one in four US adults did NOT read even one book that year.*

So here's what I know, you are 76% of the US population. If you actually commit and finish this book, you are less than two in ten.

Would you like to be part of the minority who understands the benefit of follow-through and finishing what she started? I sure hope so.

And if you don't have it in you, maybe some old-fashioned competition will have inspired you to be part of the very, very, very small minority of winners. (See what I just did there?)

Unfortunately, I've seen way too many people give up on their dreams because it's too hard or they're tired of trying.

But if you ask anyone who has ever been successful in life what their secret was, they will answer something along the lines of *perseverance*.

---

* https://www.cnbc.com/2019/01/29/24-percent-of-american-adults-havent-read-a
-book-in-the-past-year--heres-why-.html)

They never gave up. They decided to keep on trying. They believed in their dreams more than anyone else. Because guess what? Only YOU can convince yourself to get out of bed when your heart has been broken...again. Only YOU can decide that 'the one' is still out there regardless of how much you just want to curl up into a ball and die.

Today the journey begins towards Happily Ever After.

Actually, that's a lie.

The journey began the day you were born.

But more accurately - the conscious journey towards Happily Ever After begins today. Because now you're a helluva lot smarter than you were in the past. You've got some battle scars and a bruised heart. But you're deciding to continue onward, no matter what, because you believe in True Love and you KNOW you deserve your own fairy tale.

And I'm right there with ya!

You deserve it, and you can have it.

But do you have the "oomph!" needed actually to follow through with the desires in your heart?

Do you have the cajones to go after your dreams with the tenacity of a dateless cheerleader a week before prom?

Because THAT is what you've got to do.

And it doesn't have to be difficult. Or even unpleasant.

This entire journey can be...FUN!

Yup.

I'm a big fan of having fun in life. No matter what.

This week allow your intention to be to have fun as you explore your past heartaches. I'll be asking you to reflect and journal quite a bit this week.

Why?

Because if you don't understand your history, you are bound to repeat it. Over and over again, my dear.

Without further ado, let's jump in! And I fully expect to see you emerge victorious on the other side, my seventeen percenter!

Day 1
Yeah, But What Do You Want?

> "Lame, vague goals are the best
> way to live a lame, vague life."
> **—Jen Sincero**

Most of my clients are women. And when I ask them what they want, it's usually something along the lines of:

"Oh, I don't know. I want a man who is good to me. He's got money and a job. He understands me, and I can be completely myself with him, I guess."

Do you see the problem here?

When I ask my clients what they want, if they are not able to tell me EXACTLY what they want with so much passion and heart and soul that I stand up and applaud with tears of joy running down my face, I know exactly why they are not getting what they want.

You, yes you, are the one who dictates the flow of her life.

And if you don't know what you want, you ain't gonna get it, sugar.

Whereas when you know what you want precisely ... let's say... the car you've dreamed of for years. You know the color. You know the trim. The fresh leather interior...you can smell it! You feel the wind blowing through your hair when the windows are down. You've done your research and know the exact costs and your monthly payments down to the T.

Do you think that you are much more likely to actually achieve her goal of the NEW CAR versus another woman who simply says "I need a new car" and then does not do a damn thing towards researching the car, saving up for the car, test-driving the car, selling her current car and THEN actually purchasing the car?

YES - of course you are!

Similar to buying a new car, you've got to have a clear direction and a guide towards where you want to go and what you want when you get there.

No longer is it simply allowed to desire: A man who is good to me.

That's crap. My neighbor is good to me. And he's also 80.

Today, and throughout week 1, we begin our journey with the essential process of assessing where you've been.

This includes digging into your personal family history and relationship history. It also includes understanding where you want to go. And getting crystal clear in your final destination. I want you to dig deep and pull out your inner writer. No one can answer these questions for you. Only YOU know the true desires of your heart. And if you're like many of us, you've suppressed what your heart has to say for so long with something along the lines of, *"oh, that's silly. No one makes money volunteering in Morocco for 9 months out of the year building schools."* Or, *"Who am I to want to make money doing what I love? Children are starving in Africa."*

But guess what? Whatever your heart wants is actually RIGHT and PERFECT for you. It's guiding you to the Happily Ever After you so desire. So, it's actually time, right now, to start LISTENING to your heart. (And more on that in weeks 2 and 4).

So, pull up a chair and let's get comfy, shall we? Pull out your journal and take some time to answer the following questions:

Journal Questions:

- *If you could have your absolute perfect day, what would it look like?*
- *What are some of your deepest dreams and desires that you haven't told many (if any) people regarding what you want out of life?*
- *What is the "grand finale" or "final destination" vision you have for your love life? If I could wave a magic wand and give you all of your wishes and dreams, what would it look like?*
- *What's your relationship like with your mother/step-mother?*
- *What's your relationship like with your father/step-father?*
- *What did you see in your parents' relationship growing up? What did you see/feel/hear/experience regarding love, relationships, and intimacy?*
- *What's the best positive example you've had of a healthy relationship in your life?*
- *Do you have any repeating habits or patterns in your life that you'd like to change?*
- *If you had all the money and resources you needed, what would you be doing with your life?*
- *What do you value most in life?*
- *What's your earliest childhood memory?*
- *What do you love most about the opposite sex?*
- *What drives you crazy about the opposite sex?*

Take some time to answer these questions. When you're done, I'd like you to put on your 'observational glasses' and see if you can notice any patterns or themes. For example, if you had a father who was absent growing up and you seem to always attract unavailable men or men who walk out on you...could it be perhaps that you are merely recreating a familiar feeling of an unavailable man in your life based on your earliest example of a male figure?

I know that answering these questions and learning to be the observer of your life can be challenging. You will most likely feel resistance to doing this exercise. But I promise you, the more you do the work like this, the easier it will be to see your own patterns. And once you can see your patterns, you'll be able to break them far easier!

Remember: it's not enough to answer the questions in your mind. You MUST write them down on paper. Your mind is too quick and thinks too fast, and you might miss a majority of what the subconscious is wanting to say when you take the time to write. So please do this exercise before moving on.

Fill in the blank:
I'm ready for love because _____.

Day 2

Setting Your Intention

"Intention is one of the most powerful
forces there is. What you mean when you
do a thing will always determine the outcome.
The law creates the world."

—Brenna Yovanoff

I begin every yoga class I teach by asking my students to set an intention for their practice.

Think of an intention like a purpose or a goal. Similar to driving your car across the country, if you don't have a clear idea of where you are going, you'll drive aimlessly and not get anywhere. Yes, you might see a lot of amazing sights along the way, but you will be doing little more than wandering around the country without a clear goal in mind.

So an intention is your goal of where you'd like to be.

Some might even say an intention is a desire for what you want. But an intention is slightly different from a desire.

Deepak Chopra in *The Seven Spiritual Laws of Success* says that a desire and an intention BOTH have you wanting something.

Let's say - The Love of your Life.

But the big difference is - attachment to the outcome.

A desire leaves you attached to the HOW.

It must happen this way. Johnny must be my soulmate. Please, please, please, God, make Johnny realize that I am the one.

Whereas an intention is - I desire the love of my life.

But you're allowing His Majesty to take care of the details. Why? Because as smart as you may think you are, I'm here to remind you that you are but stardust, my friend. There is a higher power greater than you that *might* know a little bit more than you.

And when you allow yourself to STOP trying to control it all, you'll be amazed at the results!

For example, have you ever wanted something really, really, really, really (like *really* badly) and then it didn't happen how you wanted it to happen?

But you actually got something BETTER!

And you couldn't help but think to yourself: *"Damn. I'm even more excited at how things worked out! Thank Goodness I didn't stay with him! I could have been married with two kids by now!"*

And that was ME in my early 20's by the way. I was so heart-broken for years after my high school sweetheart and I broke up. Fast-forward a couple of years, and I'm following my heart, studying abroad while living in Spain and bouncing around Europe on the weekends. I couldn't be happier, really! One day I cyber stalked my ex on Facebook, and he has two kids under 5 and is married! Yikes. That could have been me. And thank Goodness, it was not!

You see where I'm going here?

Life is always working out in your favor.

But you've GOT to get rid of that nasty attachment to the outcome of your desires. Set those intentions. Put them out there to the big kahuna in the sky...

And then...

Let go!

Trust!

Easier said than done, I know. But we'll work on the trust muscle.

Today, we are going to get clear on your 8-week intention. Set a 'stretch' goal. It might be a wee-bit unrealistic to set the goal of: I want to be married to the love of my life and buy a house and be pregnant with twins!

I mean, sure. Anyone that put herself out there honestly could get knocked up with a shotgun wedding in Vegas and put a down payment on a manufactured home...but is that what you really want to happen?

Perhaps instead, it might be more aligned to set an intention, like: Get over my ex. Feel massive love for myself. Start dating 'good' men who appreciate me and call me back when they say they will. Oh yeah, and if I happen to start seriously dating an amazing man, that would be the icing on the cake!

Once you write your intention, rip it out of your journal! And put it by your bed and read it every day. Or keep it in your journal and remember to read it every day.

Eye. On. The. Prize.

We set goals so that we can achieve them.

Not so that we can set them, forget about them, and feel crappy about ourselves. I've always noticed that the gym is so packed during the month of January that I can NEVER find a parking spot or a spin bike regardless of the time of day.

But I just remind myself that come February, all those resolutions will be long gone, and I'll have my pick of the spin bikes. Because everyone is home watching the latest sit-com while eating Fritos on the couch. (Do they even make Fritos anymore?)

That is NOT for you! I want you to remind yourself daily WHY you are doing what you are doing. This is especially important on the days you feel like crap, or you're overwhelmed, or there's a sale at your favorite shoe store.

It sure is easy to do the personal growth work when you feel like you're on top of the world! But the challenge is sticking to it when you feel like you've been run over by a truck. Or your Tinder date sucks. Again.

Having this intention nearby and reading it daily will come in handy. Trust me on this one.

THE HARVARD BUSINESS SCHOOL STUDY ON GOAL SETTING AND PLANNING

In the Harvard Business School MBA study on goal setting, the graduating class was asked a single question about their goals in life. The question was this:

Have you set written goals and created a plan for their attainment?

Before graduation, it was determined that:

- 84% of the entire class had set no goals at all
- 13% of the class had set written goals but had no concrete plans
- 3% of the class had both written goals and concrete plans

The results?

Well, you've likely somewhat guessed it.

10 years later, the 13% of the class that had set written goals but had not created plans, were making twice as much money as the 84% of the class that had set no goals at all.

However, the apparent kicker is that 3% of the class that had both written goals and a plan, were making ten times as much as the rest of the 97% of the class.

Now there actually is quite a bit of speculation if this study even existed. However, the point of the story (factual or not) is quite clear and can be summed up in a couple of points.

1. **Set a highly specific goal.** Instead of saying "I desire to be happy," or "I want to lose weight," clarify the number of pounds you want to lose and by when, which will ensure that you can track your progress and adjust the sails as necessary as you are cruising towards your dreams.

2. **Create strong enough reasons filled with emotion.** Have you ever wanted something really badly but not so much that when things got complicated, you decided it was too hard and just gave up? If you simply want a partner because you're tired of being alone, the emotion is not strong enough. I guarantee you'll give up after 5 horrible dates in a row. But if what you really want is a partner and a friend who has your back no matter what because you've never experienced that type of safety and security, then you're much more likely to keep going. Superficial reasons for your intention without a strong emotional backing are the recipe for failure. What's your big why here, and can you make it emotional enough so that you will keep moving towards your goal no matter what?

3. **Create a plan to achieve your goal.** And guess what? Reading this book is your plan towards achieving the love of your life! Plans don't mean you need to flesh out every step you are going to take. But there needs to be an outline in place. For example, writing this book started as a goal. I then set a date that I wanted to finish the book by in addition to daily hours that I'd be writing each day. I didn't go so far as to put down what I would be writing about each day. But simply having the intention was not enough. I had to create a plan to finish the book in a reasonable time. And you bet your sweet bottom there was plenty of emotion behind what I've done here. So that emotion fueled me to get up and write EVERY SINGLE MORNING even on those mornings that I was tired and didn't

feel like meditating and writing because I'd rather be at the beach playing in the ocean. (I took a summer-long vacation in Costa Rica and Guatemala to write this book, so I wouldn't be distracted by 'daily life.' But let me tell you, the ocean and the monkeys and the sand are certainly valid distractions.) No matter where you are at in life, there will always be distractions and reasons why you should wait until some unforeseen time in the future to put your dreams into action. These are sly tricks of the ego preventing you from having it all. You CAN have everything you desire, and YES, you will have to put forth some inspired action based on what you want.

4. **Take massive action.** And this means setting time aside every day to do the work outlined in this book. Yes, 30 to 60 minutes a day can be HUGE towards achieving your dreams. In my example, I MOVED out of my home and country for the summer so I could focus entirely on my book. Talk about massive action. But guess what? The result is in your hands.

Don't be scared to THINK BIG and ACT BIGGER when it comes to creating the life of your dreams.

Let's say your goal was to lose 20 pounds in two months. That can seem daunting! Especially when the most you've ever lost is two pounds...and then you gained five back. But, if you break that goal down, you'll realize it's 10 pounds per month and 2.5 pounds per week. If there are 3500 calories in one pound of body weight, then you're looking at 8750 calories a week or 1,250 a day. So, how can you both cut out some crappy calories every single day and boost your cardio up, so you're making up for the difference? What if your afternoon snack was always a candy bar and a soda? That's 400 calories of sugar that are NOT serving you right there. Start attending a spin class daily, and you'll be able to work off those extra 850 calories. These are two small changes to your daily life that can add up huge over 8 weeks. If you start tracking your results daily and weekly, you can adjust if something isn't working or stops working.

Intention + Inspired Action = Massive Results

I promise that if you continue to work towards your dreams, they will happen. Most likely not overnight...but you never know, do ya?

Exercise: Set An Intention

Get your fine self into a comfortable position, and I'd like you to close your eyes and focus on your breathing for one minute (set your phone timer for one minute, so you don't have to keep checking). Just breathe in and out and in and out. Nothing more than that. If thoughts try to jump into your head, push them out while focusing on the rise and fall of your belly.

After a minute of focusing on your breath, ask yourself: *What is my 8-week intention?*

Allow the answer to come to the surface of your mind without trying to force it.

Write down your 8-week intention on a sheet of paper that you can rip out of your journal and set by your bed so you can read it every day and every night.

It's not enough to simply set a goal and forget about it. One must be constantly reminded of what one wants. Plus, it simply feels good to read it every day.

To learn more about how to properly set an intention, check out the book resources at www.emyraldsinclaire.com/destinationsoulmate

Fill in the blank:
I'm ready for love because _____.

Day 3

What's Love Got To Do With It?

"What's love got to do,
got to do with it?"
—Tina Turner song

Everything!

Let me get a bit hippy-dippy on you for a moment and proclaim that love truly is at the core of everything and all things. Love thy neighbor. Love yourself. Love your ex. Love your parents who gave you up for adoption. Love the puppy who pees on your flowers.

Love can heal all pains and all grudges no matter how badly you've been hurt.

But before we can heal, we've got to do a bit of excavation into your past love life. It's never easy or fun to bring up the past, especially when the thought of it can cause you pain. But it's a necessary process, and you'll see why, later on, when we come back to this story.

Today you're going to write out your "Love Story" in full detail. You'll give me all the juicy (and sometimes painful) details. Please do not hold back. This story is 100% for your reflection and healing. Write down the good, the bad, and the ugly. It's okay if you forget some details but do your best to unearth all the painful emotions and feelings that go along with your personal Love Story.

One thing I have to mention, I personally believe that most parents are always doing the best they can with the resources and knowledge they have at the time. And yet, many still grow up with the feeling that they aren't good enough or loveable. Why does this happen? Because when you're young (and let's be honest, at every age really), you make everything out to be about yourself. So no matter how many times your parents told you they loved you, the *one time* that your mom was tired and stressed out and yelled at you, BAM! You took that moment in and created a negative story around it and it lasted with you for the rest of your life. Which is why for most of us, we don't necessarily remember all the lovey-dovey moments from childhood. Instead, the ones that stick out are the trying times and challenging moments.

For example, my Love Story would look something like this:

My parents divorced when I was three, and for as long as I can remember, there has always been animosity between them.

Most of my memories of my stepfather revolve around him being a bit of a jerk. He never seemed to listen and was extremely stubborn. After he passed, my mother actually shared with me that my stepfather really did care and was hurt that he didn't have a closer relationship with his stepchildren. That was an eye-opening moment for sure, because, as a child, I held a lot of resentment towards my stepfather. *(Could something similar be going on in your life in regards to the memories you have growing up?)*

My mother and step-father didn't seem to have a loving relationship, and as I got older, I came to resent him even more. They moved into separate bedrooms, and I declared to myself that I would NEVER continue to live with a man if we were at that state. I'd rather be alone and happy than comfortable and settling. (Once again, remember that this story is from the eyes of a young adult. And the stories I created in my mind as a result. It has nothing to do with the *reality* of what was happening between my mother and step-father. The most important thing to remember is that *you are <u>always creating stories</u>* based on what is going on around you. And there is no absolute truth. There is simply <u>*your story*</u>. And in this book we are going to create a new love story based on what you want to create instead!)

My dad is with his third wife. They seem to have a healthy relationship. Growing up, I spent time with my dad and my step-mom for holidays and vacations. I remember traveling quite a bit with them and honestly don't remember too much about his relationship with his second wife. Many stories came out later on that had me wondering, *hmm... maybe that's where I get that from.* As a child, you're taking everything in and creating a story around it. And so even though I don't remember everything in crystal clear detail, I know the relationship my dad had with his second wife affected me in many ways

When I think of a super positive example of a loving relationship from childhood, I remember my best friend Tim Baldwin. His house was always filled with laughter, and I loved spending time there because his parents were always touching and seemed genuinely happy with each other. I specifically remember one moment when Tim's mom told me that relationships are a lot of hard work, and you have to give more than you receive but that it's worth it. And, that was their secret to being together for so long and being so happy. What she said to me stuck with me to this day. Yes, you can have a happy and fun-filled relationship. And yes, it will take some work, compromise and effort.

The first love of my life was named Patrick. In high school, Patrick and I dated for about a year. He was my first everything, and I was smitten with him. I thought we'd be together forever. But eventually, the magic started to fade, and we began to fight. A lot. And it seemed like I was always in a pissy mood. And as I became more bitch-like, Patrick pulled away. I didn't feel loved or appreciated by him. I seriously considered breaking up with him, but I loved him so much I could not. Instead, on a crazy drunken night, we got in a fight at a party, and I cheated on him.

I never felt so horrible in my entire life, and I battled my conscience for a week before my best friend said I had to tell him.

He immediately broke up with me, and I was crushed. I cried myself to sleep for MONTHS. I stopped eating. I was severely depressed. I tried to apologize and win him back. But he had already moved on and found another woman. (Years later they are married with three kids as far as I know!) It took me months to recover and heal. I've since forgiven myself for my actions and know it was all working out perfectly in my favor. He was not *the one*, but he was a huge part of my journey.

That scar of betraying his trust stayed with me for years in the form of building walls around my heart and my fear of being open and vulnerable. It also affected my self-worth. It would take me YEARS to build that back up again.

My next serious relationship in high school ended when he went away to college. I was scared to admit my feelings, and he never once told me he loved me. After almost a year of dating, I inquired as to if he wanted to stay together and date long distance. He told me no. I acted like it was no big deal and continued to have sex with him anyway. I felt like crap. I felt so low. I had low self-worth and no skills to stand up for myself.

Fast forward to college, for lack of a better term, I became a whore for love. I slept around. A lot. And not because I loved sex and wanted it all the time. It was because I thought, for some strange reason, that if I slept with a man, he would want to be with me. I was trying (unsuccessfully) to use sex as a way to capture a man's heart.

I can tell you it didn't work. And I tried quite a few times. I even tried dating a woman to see if that would be any different. But guess what happened? I got scared. I didn't open my heart. I cheated on her, and she broke up with me instantly. She and her mom dropped me off at the train station, and she didn't look back or say one word to me. I felt like a royal butt-head for hurting her. To this day, I've still never spoken to her. And to this day, I have massive respect for her for standing up for herself like that.

After college was B. What a strange ride that was. An open relationship for years because both of us were scared of commitment. I know I wanted a man to love and cherish me completely. I wanted to dive deep. But I also was not ready for it. And so I said 'ok' when this man 15 years my senior wanted to be with me...but also wanted an open, long-distance relationship. We danced together for almost five years before I realized that I could have more. I could have it all.

And then...Tim. *Sigh.* Tim was who I thought was 'The One.' He was the Wesley to my Princess Buttercup. We had such passionate sex and chemistry and fire. We could not be in the same room as each other without being glued to one another. We talked for hours on the phone. We made passionate love whenever we were together. And we seemed to be in great alignment.

The only trouble was...Tim was just getting out of a divorce and wasn't ready to commit. At this stage in my journey, I was becoming a much stronger human being and able to ask Tim flat-out what he wanted in a relationship and how he saw us moving on together in the future.

He said that he didn't know but that he wanted to see where it goes. But that he wasn't looking for something really serious at the moment.

In hindsight, why didn't I run? I knew I wanted Happily Ever After, and I wanted it with him. In not so many words, he said he wasn't ready. And so I allowed him to string me on and for myself to fall deeper and deeper in love with him.

We were on and off for six months as I would step into my power and declare that we couldn't do this, and I deserved more.

However, my strength in myself didn't last, and months later, we were making love in front of the fire.

But... eventually, I broke it off with him and fell into a mess of tears on the floor. I deserved more. I deserved it all. And I was finally standing up for myself. I knew the longer it continued onward, the harder it would become to break it off.

We had one more stint together. In which my heart fell for him one last time. And I thought it was going to be different.

But guess what happened? Tim faded away. He slowly stopped responding to my texts and calling me (I was living in Ecuador, and he was in the US). I took the hint and stopped reaching out to him, thinking, "If he wanted to be with me, he'd reach out."

Six months later, he did reach out to inquire how I was doing. I lashed out angrily. Finally, able to express all the hurt and anger I had felt because I wasn't able to speak my truth and was intimidated (yet again) by an older man I was in love with.

He was engaged and in love and oh-so-happy. Fuck You, I believe I told him.

So what happened next? The hurt of Tim is when I finally decided to get my shit together. I enrolled in plenty of on-line courses centered around love and finding the one. I read self-help books and studied with the masters. I was so done with being hurt time and time again. And with Tim, it was the first time I had actually opened my heart 100% since Patrick in high school. And the result? It was torn out of my chest and smashed into a million pieces. Weren't things supposed to be different this time because I was acting differently?

That pain prompted a huge quest within (and without) for love. What was I doing wrong, and what did I need to change?

The next year was HUGE personal growth, and while I had a couple slip-ups (aka one-night stands) that year, I also learned to stand up for myself and set massive boundaries that I never had before.

When the next man stepped into my life and told me that he wanted to be monogamous with me and 'go the distance,' I was able to honestly and clearly say 'No, thank you. I'm dating other men. I'm not sleeping around, but I'm not ready to commit to you.' And I wasn't. I didn't know him well enough. And he loved the challenge. It took him almost six months to win me over and get me to commit. And all the while, I was speaking my truth. I was honest with him, and I was almost challenging him to stop seeing me. And you know what? When that relationship ended, it wasn't the end of the world. I was 100% open with who I was. I wanted him to see the 'real me,' and if he didn't like it, then he could leave, thank you very much.

My ability to be the real me is what made all the difference. With so many men in the past, I was clingy. I had this attitude of "Are you the one? Are you the love of my life?" while on my quest. Looking back, I can see that I was attached to every single man in the past. I was needy. I needed them to be "The One" and to provide me with the love I so desperately craved.

But once I reached the point of working on myself and loving me the most, the neediness faded away. I was able to tell my man clearly that I needed space to be me and honestly decide if I wanted his companionship in my life.

Talk about a 180-degree change.

And this was the first relationship where I felt ZERO FEAR about my man leaving me. ZERO FEAR about what-ifs or the future. Because I love myself MORE than anyone else in my life. I love myself more than my man and more than our relationship. And that feeling is the most powerful, safe, and secure feeling in the entire world. I know that no matter what, I've got me, babe. And you know what, when that relationship ended, it wasn't the end of the world. We talked it out like two mature human beings, and to this day, we are still friends. And by recognizing that *that* relationship was no longer in alignment with my personal growth and goals, I made space for something so much greater.

And I know THAT is what attracted my amazing partner to me today. I could write an entire book on the Love Story of my man and I, so to keep it brief, I'll just say this:

We support each other's mutual growth both inside of the relationship and outside of it. We are both complete on our own. We have done the work, and we *desire* to be together. We do not *need* to be together. It's a mature relationship focused around holding each other accountable to be our best selves.

And honestly, life is simply better with him by my side. All of my relationships and my entire Love Story has led me to where I am today. In hindsight, I'm able to see my growth and how every relationship (and everything I experienced and saw growing up) was necessary to bring me to the relationship I am in today. I don't regret anything. But I'm going to be honest with you, it did take a while to reframe my Love Story and to forgive and let go of my past. And I want you to start that journey today. You are not the victim of your past. Your past brought you to where you are today. And from this day forward, you get to choose where you are headed.

Now it's your turn to write your Love Story.

Exercise: Your Love Story

Write your love story. Make sure to write in all the painful details and reflections as you notice them.

Make sure to bookmark this page in the journal because we are going to come back to your 'love story' in week 6.

Fill in the blank:
I'm ready for love because _____.

Day 4

Making Space For
What You Want

"When you let go of what no longer serves you,
you make space for what's meant to be."

- Unknown

et's play pretend for a moment, shall we?

Let's pretend that you had your eye on a new living room set for quite a while. Yours is old and tattered and actually something you got in your 20s at a garage sale. You're not super proud of it and actually always have your couch covered in a blanket or sheet so that people can't actually see how ratty it looks.

So you've been saving up to buy this fantastic dark leather set, and you already picked out the pillows at Pier 1 that are going to along with this fantastic new addition to your living room. You've taken the measurements and know that it's going to fit perfectly in your space, and you're super pumped, to say the least.

The day arrives when you've saved enough money and purchased the furniture, and TODAY is the day that it arrives!

You're pacing around your home in excitement. You're now considering paint options that would look better and other various ways to 'spice up' your home now that a new glamorous furniture set is on the way.

The doorbell rings.

'They are here!' you think to yourself.

You throw open the door in giddy excitement and confirm that, yes, they are indeed here with the new set. They ask where you want it.

You turn around and...

Realize the old set is STILL in the living room.

Doh!

Where is the new set going to go if the old set is still in the living room?

And that, my dear, is about a clear of an example I can give you as to why you've got to clear out the physical clutter in your love life if you want to be able to accept in your new lover.

Physical items do hold an energetic resonance to them, and they could be blocking your new love from entering your life.

And similar to the analogy of the old furniture blocking the entrance of the new furniture, items like a former boyfriend's sweatshirt that you still wear to bed at night, or photos of ex's laying around, or gifts from past lovers always on your mantle are blocking the entrance of your new love.

Today's exercise is quite simple. You are going to look around your home and look for ways that 'physical clutter' is getting in the way of your Prince Charming being there.

Is the nightstand on his side of the bed completely covered in books and papers and a couple of glasses of water? Or is it completed cleared and available for the love of your life to place his stuff on it, like a phone and charger and Chapstick?

Is your passenger car seat a complete mess and overflowing with your purse, and running shoes and workout clothes and makeup bag?

Or do you consciously keep it clear knowing that he will need a space to sit when he arrives?

Taking these simple actions can create a substantial energetic shift.

When I was preparing for my partner, I cleared out my home, my car, and even my workspace! I wanted to make sure that I was putting the correct message out to the universe ... that there was actually room in my life for my lover to step in. And not only that, I was so confident that he was on his way that I was already cleaning up and preparing for him!

You see how important of a message it sends when you physically start moving stuff around and clearing out the clutter?

Exercise: Clean Out The Physical Clutter

Places to consider:

Living Room (Is your space clean and inviting for someone else?)

Bedroom (Do you have space for another person in your room to enjoy a comfortable sleep and feel welcome?)

Bathroom (Do you have girly stuff everywhere, or could another human being leave personal items behind and feel good using the bathroom?)

Refrigerator (Is your fridge a mess? Is it filled with takeout boxes and leftovers? Or is it filled with fresh ingredients and ready for making meals with your beloved?)

Car (Is your passenger seat ready to accept another person? Instead of throwing your purse on the passenger seat the next time you get in, why not put it in the backseat instead and visualize that your man will be seated next to you soon?)

Workspace (Think about how your work environment will be affected once he arrives. Make it clean and presentable, something you would be proud of showing off. Is there a particular guy at work that you're always flirting with (that you know won't go anywhere) that you need to stop doing so now because your guy certainly wouldn't appreciate seeing that when he surprises you at the office!

Things to consider getting rid of:

- Gifts from ex's or his/her family
- Items left behind from past lovers
- Photos of you and previous partners

Other Considerations:

Do you have time in your life for a partner? Do you work too much? Is your social schedule already full of your volunteer activities?

What's your roommate situation like? I once worked with a woman who was renting out her basement to a middle-aged man. She quickly realized that it was blocking her ability to attract a man who wanted to move in and commit to her because another man was already taking that 'space' and barring him from coming in.

Fill in the blank:

I'm ready for love because _____.

Day 5

Clearing Out The Clutter

"Once your mindset changes, everything on
the outside will change along with it."
- Steve Maraboli

Today we are going to build on yesterday's practice of clearing
out the clutter in your life.

And today will be so much more difficult than yesterday
because today we are cleaning out your mind!

Your mind is a powerful tool of creation, allowing you to experience
all your dreams made manifest...or it's a trap holding you prisoner to
your greatest fears.

When I ask a woman why she is single, I will get a variety of
responses such as:

There are no good men in my town.
All the good ones are taken.
Dating is very difficult in my town.
I already know everyone in town.
I'm too old/fat/stupid/tall/spiritual/picky for the men around here.

And while the mind (and you) can easily find logical and rational proof to support these claims, they are absolutely not based on truth.

It's a mindset that gets reinforced based on your perception of reality.

And you create a belief around it. Because you believe it, your eyes are trained to see what you believe (even if this is a subconscious belief), and so you see it again and again and again.

Just like the racist who thinks all Mexicans are not to be trusted, he will always encounter those from Mexico who lie, cheat, and steal.

But the person who wakes up on the right side of the bed and declares "today is going to be the best day ever!" will most likely run into happy people, experience 'lucky encounters,' and have men go out of their way to open doors for her.

This is really important to reiterate again, so I'll repeat it.

Your thoughts create your reality. And NOT the other way around. Because you believe something, you will see it. And your perception of what you see is based on your belief system. That means you will only see that which you believe you will see.

For example, there's a fantastic story of a man who ran his car into an airplane in the middle of the road.

The plane had to perform an emergency landing in the middle of Nebraska (or somewhere out there). The plane landed, and everyone was safe. Yea! But the man out driving his car in the middle of the night did not SEE the plane.

What?

How could you not see a massive 737 in the middle of the road when there is nothing else in sight?!

His mind did not see it because he wasn't expecting to see it!

There's another story portrayed in the movie (and book) *What the Bleep Do We Know?* It tells of the Native Americans in North American not being able to see the ships of Columbus because they had never seen anything like that before. Their minds were not prepared to see something that they had never seen or experienced before.

BUT...

They could see the waves hitting the shore. And so the elders sat on the shore, and they stared, and they stared, and they stared. They knew something had to be out there because they could see the waves crashing on the beach that reflected a vessel of some sort on the water.

And then one day - bam! One of the elders saw the ships of Columbus, and as if by magic, everyone else could see them too.

The thoughts you have around love and what you believe you are capable of receiving are a direct reflection of what you are experiencing in your life.

So today, we are going to clear out the mental clutter.

I'd like you to start by making a list of all of your fears around love. Start by freewriting with the prompt:

I'm most scared of...

Exercise: I'm Most Scared Of...

Being alone, dying alone, never finding true love, never having that partner to share the little things with.

From there, I'd like you to brain dump all of your negative belief systems around love.

For example: There are no good men in my town. I'll always be alone. I'm too fat to be asked out. I'm not good enough. I'm too stupid. I am in debt, and no man wants a woman in debt. Men are intimidated by my smarts.

Once you've done, pat yourself on the back! This is a huge part of your transformation. You've just faced the beast head-on. Good job, you. That wasn't so bad, was it?

Look over your list and for each item say out loud: *I forgive myself for thinking this way. I choose to see love instead.*

41

You don't have to (yet) believe it. But it's an essential first step in letting go of the mental clutter that gets in your way.

In the second step, for the next 24 hours, I'd like you to become aware of the 'mental clutter.' What are the stories that automatically pop into your head as you go about your day?

If you catch yourself caught up in the clutter, say to yourself, *I forgive myself for having this thought. I choose to see love instead.*

Fill in the blank:

I'm ready for love because _____.

Day 6

More Cleansing Work

"Stop being afraid of what could go wrong and start being excited about what could go right."
—Tony Robbins

I was once working with an Indian woman. And in her culture, a woman is usually married by 26. After 26, she's almost a hopeless case and starts to worry about living with her parents forever.

It's their culture.

So when she reached out to me at 26, she was worried she'd be alone forever.

Those of you in Europe or North American might laugh at her concerns. Many women have careers and don't actually think about a family and settling down until their 30s or even their 40s!

But in her mind, if she is not married by 27, she is done for because of her religion and her culture.

I was working with another client, Kalie. Kalie was in a horribly abusive relationship with a man who clearly did not love and cherish her. He always talked about other women in front of Kalie and told her she was stupid and that he didn't want to have sex with her. And yet she stayed with him. Why? Because she was a Catholic and a 'good Catholic girl' does not get divorced.

In this case, religion was preventing her from doing what is the healthiest thing, which was to leave her husband.

Now, turn the mirror on yourself. In what ways are your current religious beliefs, along with cultural/societal/familial norms creating certain mental blocks in your mind as to what you can have, be or do?

Now I'm not saying you should change your religion or run away from home and never speak to your parents again on your quest for love.

But I am suggesting that you get really clear on what it is that you really believe versus beliefs that have simply been handed to you that you take for granted.

Exercise: Clearing Out The Spiritual And Cultural Clutter

Make a list of all the ways that religion or society is preventing you from being open to love. This includes anything that makes you feel anxious or within a lacking mentality around love.

For example:

I cannot divorce this man.
If I'm not married by 28, I'll be a spinster forever.
I cannot have a successful career and a healthy marriage.
I cannot marry a man outside of my religion.

Once your list is complete, look it over. Which of the items truly resonates with you? Which ones do you actually believe to be true for you?

It can be tricky to pull apart our own belief systems from those that have been handed to us. But this step right here is usually an eye-opening one for many!

Next to each item on your list, write the following: **Through love, all things are possible**.

And then I want you to feel the possibility that through love, all things are possible.

Fill in the blank:

I'm ready for love because _____.

Day 7
Day Off

"There is a virtue in work and a virtue in rest.
Use both and overlook neither."
—Alan Cohen

Today is a free day. I want you to look back upon your journaling
from the last week. Look at how far you've already come in
only six days. You've done a lot regarding CLEARING out your
life and MAKING SPACE for the love you desire.

Congrats, my dear.

Today, make sure you go and do something for you to celebrate.
I'm a big fan of celebrating all the little things because they add up to
the big things eventually. Buy yourself flowers, take a walk-through
nature, get some gelato, watch a sunset with yourself. Whatever it is
that allows you to celebrate your progress for the week.

Week 2

A DREAM
IS A WISH
YOUR HEART
MAKES...

"Tell me what you want, what you really, really, want."

—The Spice Girls

Oh. Emm. Gee.

Remember the Spice Girls?

I totally wanted to be 'Baby Spice.' She was cute, innocent, and approachable.

And yet at the same time, I envied "Posh Spice," aka Victoria Beckham, because let's be real, she screamed "Sex Appeal!" And let's not forget "Sporty Spice" who was actually a much better representation of little me at that time who was more obsessed with soccer and swimming than I was with manicures and hair-cuts.

What did my little heart really want?

Well, everything to be honest.

I wanted to be cute and sexy AND sporty.

And as I grew up, that never changed. My desires increased, and it moved on to wanting to study international business and travel the world. I managed a branch of a house-painting company while in college and made quite a bit of money. Enough to live and study in Spain for a year while tromping through Europe.

And I have another side to me. I am open-minded, spiritual, and into yoga. I wanted to know WHY the body worked the way it did and how food affects our body. And so I became a nutritionist. And I got my yoga certification. And I moved to Ecuador and managed a retreat center for most of my twenties.

I didn't have any of this planned out in advance. I simply followed my heart and KNEW that I could have anything I desired. If I put my mind to it. And BELIEVED it could happen.

This is the marriage between old-school and new-age.

Old-School: believing things like 'the early bird gets the worm,' and 'if I work harder, I'll make more money and accomplish my dreams.'

New-Age: believing in the 'power of intention.' and affirmations and manifesting things into existence.

I'm here to tell you that it's a little bit of both. Knowing what you want and then ACTING on your dreams and desires is the best way I know to create the life of your dreams.

But if you don't know what you want or have been too scared to admit to yourself that what you really want to do is be a librarian, or an actress, or to build a school in Africa, then you will never take inspired action towards those dreams.

And the love of your life is only a part of your dreams.

You know the expression that relationships are 50/50?

Well, that is crap.

You do NOT complete me, Jerry Maguire.

A healthy, happy, and spiritual relationship is two WHOLES coming together.

A man does not fix you, save you or complete you, little missy.

The time is NOW to get clear on the life you want. It has nothing to do with what your parents want for you. It certainly has nothing to do with societal norms. And for the moment, let's put aside the potential compromise and merging of lives that happens when you meet 'the one.' Instead, let's focus on little ol' you and what your beautiful heart wants if you truly could 'have it all.'

As my dad always told me growing up: If you don't believe you can have it all, you get to choose how much less than it all you get to have.

So, let's have it all, shall we?

Truly unraveling and understanding your heart's desires is the first step to actually getting what you want! This week, you'll learn with absolute certainty WHO you are, WHAT you desire, and HOW to get it. And when it comes to finding Prince Charming...this is the most crucial step to take to draw him that much closer to you.

Let's have our cake and eat it too, shall we?

Day 1

Your Five Closest Friends

> "You're the average of the five people
> you spend the most time with."
> **—Jim Rohn**

Have you ever heard the expression that you are the average of the five people you hang out with the most?

If not, it's about time.

The people that you hang out with the most influence your way of thinking and what you actually believe is possible in your life.

If you're hanging out with those who all have minimum wage jobs, zero direction in life, and would rather spend their free time lounging on the couch smoking a bong, then you are most likely NOT going to strive to do anything bigger than perhaps saving up for a bigger bong.

If, on the other hand, you are hanging out with entrepreneurs who have big goals and dreams and expansive minds, they are going to support your dreams and encourage you and remind you that anything is possible. To them, failure is not the end of the world. It's merely a gift or a lesson for learning.

If we become the average of the five people we hang out with the most, how do we quickly and easily change our external environment?

For one, you can change the people you hang out with. Instead of going out with the single ladies and complaining about the loser men in your town, I invite you to hang out with your married friends and ask them for advice about being happy. Mix it up and go to a gallery opening (if that excites you) or something that gets you out of your comfort zone!

For two, you can actually nourish MORE sides of you and become the average of five different sides of you.

Before you scream, "Schizophrenia!" I invite you to allow me to explain.

We are multi-faceted human beings with multiple sides. I, for example, am a yogi, an athlete, a writer, a speaker, an activist, an animal lover, an extrovert, an introvert, a chef, a foodie, a photographer, an actress, and so much more.

But at any given moment, I am not honoring all of those sides of me at once. It's not possible. But if I were to pick the top five that I genuinely want to embody at any given moment, it might be something like this:

1. The Optimist who always believes that life is working for her and everything is perfect and that I am blessed.

2. The Learner who is continually striving to grow her brain, improve her situation, and take lessons from what's happening around her.

3. The Lover who believes in Happily Ever After and sucks every last drop of nectar out of the beauty and romance of life.

4. The Extrovert who loves meeting new people and going to events and striking up a conversation.

5. The Teacher who absolutely loves to share her knowledge base with others in an effort to be the change and spark a new way of thought in another.

From there, I would plan out my week and ask myself how I can honor all five of those sides of me. The optimist might read an uplifting book on the power of positivity. The learner could go to a class or enroll in a series of classes. The lover might take time to go to the hot springs or indulge in a bubble bath with candles. The extrovert could go to a networking event and see how many heart-felt connections she could make. And the teacher would undoubtedly get herself in front of the camera and create educational videos for her following.

So I ask you — who are you? Who are you today? Who do you desire to be in the future? What sides of yourself are you NOT honoring that you'd like to?

Grab your journal and complete the following exercise:

Exercise: Honoring All Sides of You

Make a list of all sides of you. It's ok if you aren't actively utilizing a certain side of yourself. For example, I have a history of acting, and I would call myself an actress. However, I cannot tell you the last time I performed on stage. But it's still a side of me that I'd put on the list.

For example: businesswoman, yogi, mother, sister, poet, activist, animal lover

I also want you to make a list of the person you would like to be that you don't feel like you truly are yet.

Exercise: Honoring Future You

For example: writer, world-renowned speaker, thought-leader, business owner, mother

Then review your list. If you could pick five people to hang out with, what traits would they employ? Circle the top five from your lists.

From there, grab your schedule, and over the next week, I'd like you to pick five ways to embody those five traits that you'd like to become or simply nourish more.

If you'd like to become a writer, make time to sit down and write.

If you'd like to become a speaker, make time to practice talking in front of the camera or look up various organizations where you can speak for free.

If you'd like to become a mother, what do you need to learn NOW about being a mom while you have time to dedicate to the learning process?

We truly can change our lives by changing the people we hang out with. But it doesn't have to be external. The work always starts from within. Once you start embodying the person you'd like to be and the life you'd like to have, the external world will change to reflect that. And you will automatically start to attract different people into your life that will help you to become even more of that person.

Fill in the blank:

I love myself because _____.

Day 2

The Love List

"Beauty begins the moment you
decide to be yourself."
—Coco Chanel

I s there a magical way to ensure that you feel happy every single day?

Not that I know of.

However, there is a tool that I use called the Love List that can surely help to guarantee positivity and love every single day of your life. And what could be better than that?

You cannot control every single situation in your life. In fact, I would go so far as to wager that you can control NO situation in your life.

But what you CAN control is your reaction to every situation that life throws your way.

When your plane is delayed, are you pissed off and angry at the inconvenience? Or do you choose to use the time as a way to catch up on a book you've been meaning to read?

When you're stuck in traffic, are you annoyed and frustrated? Or do you take the opportunity to turn on your favorite podcast and learn some new information?

When your favorite yoga teacher has a sub, do you decide to no longer take the class because you love her style? Or do you use it as a way to potentially find a new yoga instructor that you adore and learn how to move your body differently?

The only thing we will ever have control of in our lives is our reaction to any situation.

But I'm not Buddha, and I'm not perfect. Sometimes I do get pissed off and annoyed. Some days I feel sad and hopeless. And still, other days, I don't want to do much more than lay in a hammock out in the sun instead of working behind my computer.

These are all parts of being a human being.

However, you can also stack the deck in your favor if you'd like to improve your state of mind and attract more wonderful things into your life.

Like attracts like.

Ever heard that before?

If you're a self-help addict, like me, you have heard a variation of it before. So if you find yourself consistently down in the dumps and struggling to find reasons to be hopeful and happy on any given day because your reality does not match what you'd actually like it to be, I have an enjoyable exercise for you.

It's called the "Love List," and it's been designed to help your beautiful self to stay in high-vibration and a happy-go-lucky state most of the time!

How does that sound?

Exercise: The Love List

Put out your journal and number a page (or two) from 1 to 30. Then next to each number, write down one thing that puts you in a good mood. They can be big things for little things such as: going to the beach, traveling, reading, taking a bath, reading a good book, cooking, laughing with friends.

Then, your goal, little missy, is to make sure that every day for the next 30 days, you are doing something on that list!

It doesn't have to be everything on the list. But the point is that at least once a day every day you are putting yourself first. You are filling your own love cup up! And this helps to put you in a joyous and happy mood every single day.

And as a special bonus, when you're feeling down or upset, you can refer to your Love List and give yourself a little kick in the rear and make yourself go do something on that list knowing that you're going to feel better afterward.

Like Attracts Like, remember?

And a negative Nancy who is down in the dumps will NOT attract a powerful, loving and supportive man. It just is not how the Universe works. We live in an attraction-based universe, which is the premise of the Law of Attraction.

It's time today, beauty, to step into your power and take control of your feelings and your happiness and your life. And it starts by simply being aware of what RAISES your vibration and making sure you are doing those things every single day.

Easy peasy, huh?!

Fill in the blank:
I love myself because _____.

Day 3

Accept Yourself

"If you don't take care of your body,
where are you going to live?"
—Saw it on a shirt

The common trait or belief that I notice across the board with my clients is the belief that "I'm not good enough."

As human beings (and certainly growing up in the United States of America), we are consistently taught to grow and strive to change. What we have is certainly not enough. Instead, we need bigger, shinier, better...and certainly more expensive than what we have.

The magazines are filled with photoshopped beauty models, while drug-addiction and substance abuse run wildly out of control!

I want you to know that you are not alone in your feelings of inadequacy. We all have them. Myself included. Why else do you think I've made it my life's mission to live love, be love, and spread love? I've got my own feelings of inadequacy to overcome.

Armed with the information that none of us truly feel like we are good enough, you now have the power to shift those feelings. And it's not a huge mountain that you have to climb. Instead, it's a simple exercise I learned from Louise Hay

Exercise: The Mirror Exercise

Go to the mirror. (Yup, right now.)

Look yourself in the eye and say: I love and accept myself right now.

And now repeat it.

And again.

And again.

Say it at least 10 times.

Say it until you cry.

Say it even if you feel like a complete whack job.

And now throughout your day whenever you catch a glance of yourself in the mirror or a window that you walk by, instead of berating yourself (as so many of us do) and picking yourself apart, whisper (or say silently in your head), *I love and accept myself right now.*

Do this every single day for the rest of your life. Or at least until you start to believe it.

Typically it takes about 10 to 14 days for my clients to note that they actually notice a change in the sound of their voice when they say it. To me, that is when your body actually starts to believe this new way of thinking.

Love yourself.

Accept yourself.

Exactly as you are right now.

There is nothing you need to change. Right now, you are perfect. You are lovely. You are precisely who you are supposed to be, and everything that has happened in your life was (and is) perfectly orchestrated.

It actually might take a while for you to believe what I just wrote above. But trust me on this one, you can fake it 'til you make it.

Here are some common side effects of instant self-love and self-acceptance:

- Unexpected happiness.
- Unwavering optimism.
- The feeling that 'everything is always working out for me.'
- The desire to laugh for no reason.
- Love and appreciation for your body.
- A boost in self-confidence.
- Feeling like you can move mountains...and then going out and actually doing so!
- Standing firm in your power and making no apologies for who you are.
- The desire to share love and positivity with every single person you meet.

You got this, babe!

Fill in the blank:
I love myself because _____.

Day 4

Your Ideal Love Life

"If you can dream it, you can do it."
—Walt Disney

When you were a child, did you ever close your eyes and dream?

Did you ever get lost in your imagination and spend hours playing outside, imagining you were a fairy princess on some grand adventure? Was there magic and mystery and excitement around every corner?

Were you so lost in the story that you never even heard your parents calling you for dinner?

When I was a child, I would literally spend HOURS outside playing in the forest. I was an explorer searching for new lands (and salamanders) behind the barn. Or I was a princess trapped in a tower, but I escaped! And now I was staying ahead of the bad guy and quickly searching for a way out of the swamp and towards my freedom.

And no, I never heard my parents the first time (or the second) when they called me for dinner.

I was lost in my made-up world of adventure and fun.

So what if I asked you to close your eyes and pretend you were that little kid again? And I asked you to imagine your ideal love life, what would it look like?

What details could you conjure up in your mind? What adventures would the two of you take together? What type of feelings would come up for you in your body? Can you keep your eyes closed and get lost in the story for a while?

I hope so because this is precisely what I'm asking you to do today.

Too often when we 'grow up,' we are told to become realistic. That's not possible, they say. But who are they to be the decision-makers in your destiny?

Alice laughed: *"There's no use trying,"* she said; *"one can't believe impossible things."*

"I daresay you haven't had much practice," said the Queen. *"When I was younger, I always did it for half an hour a day. Why sometimes I've believed as many as six impossible things before breakfast."*

Today is the day you get to harness the power of your imagination. We are given our imagination for a reason. The imagination is your source of creation. It's the only way you're ever going to change your current situation. Anyone can look around at their present reality and choose to see their present reality. As a result, that person gets more of the same.

But think of the person who chooses to see a completely different reality instead.

Martin Luther King Jr. had a dream.

Gandhi saw peace in a world of war.

Steve Jobs envisioned a completely different way of people interacting with one another.

None of these visions was ever a present reality. Instead, what was strong was their vision of a future reality. And the fact that they didn't let anyone else tell them it was not possible. They spent more time in their imagined future than they did in the present moment.

And that is what has made all the difference, my love.

Pull out your journal and imagine your perfect love life. Do not hold back. Write the big things and the little things. There is nothing wrong that you can write, as long as it's what your heart truly desires.

Exercise: Your Ideal Love Life

What's true in your heart is true for you.

When you've completed writing your ideal love life, close your eyes and spend a minute or two basking in the feeling of it actually happening. Allow every cell of your body to experience this new reality that is on its way to you.

It's important to note that this exercise is not something you do once. Martin Luther King Jr. did not have a dream and then push it aside. He had a dream, and it stayed at the front of his mind, always. He spoke it. He breathed it. He taught it. He believed it. He lived it.

It's time for you to start living your dream. Every single day.

So keep this exercise somewhere handy where you can read it and feel it every single day.

Fill in the blank:

I love myself because _____.

Day 5

Your Ideal Life

"First, think. Second, dream.
Third, believe. And finally, dare."
—Walt Disney

Yesterday you wrote your ideal love life and closed your eyes
and FELT it as though it were coming true.

Every single time I've done that exercise, it has worked for me!
Why?

Because I was READY. And I was sick and tired of the pain. And,
as a result, I put a LOT of feeling and emotion into what I was desiring.
And within weeks, I met a man who was 90% or more of what I had
been dreaming up!

So if this type of creation works for your love life, reason goes that
it must work for your life in general, too!

What are the mental limitations holding you back from your true
desires? As far as I'm concerned, you've got one go around in this body
to be/do/have everything that lights your heart up with joy. The time

is NOW to have everything you want and more! Quit making your excuses or putting off your dreams for some future moment in time.

Instead, you are going to paint a picture of your ideal LIFE! It's time to expand upon what you wrote yesterday and get lost in your hopes and dreams of a life that fills YOUR heart up with joy.

For some people, a life spent traveling would do it for them.

For another, simply being the best mom she can be is enough.

Maybe you want to be a race car driver. Perhaps you want to learn 20 languages. There really are no wrong answers. Instead, I invite you to close your eyes and ask your heart:

What do I want?

Take a couple of minutes with your eyes closed and meditate on that question.

You can't get what you want if you don't know what you want.

And I assure you, the answer to this question will change and evolve over time. So it's a good idea to ask yourself this question several times per week.

Give yourself permission to HAVE dreams and to go after them!

Exercise: Your Ideal Life

Set your phone timer for 2 minutes.

Put your hands on your heart and ask yourself: *What do I want?*

Then close your eyes and breathe and see yourself living the life of your dreams!

When the timer goes off, start journaling immediately and put pen to paper what your heart truly desires!

When you're done, say aloud:

I now give myself permission to make choices that feel aligned with my deepest intentions! I forgive myself for any time I have not made choices that support my deepest desires. I forgive others who may have held me back, even without meaning to do so, and I now choose to be discerning in my choices so that I create my life experience as I most desire and intend it to be. So be it!

Fill in the blank:

I love myself because _____.

Day 6

I Am The Prize

"She remembered who she was,
and the game changed."

—Lalah Deliah

Woo!! I'm so excited about today. We are wrapping up week 2 with a powerful and challenging exercise meant to help boost your self-confidence and self-love so that you step into the empowered version of yourself who actually BELIEVES that she can have everything her heart desires!

If you haven't figured it out by now, allow me to recap an essential fact. If you don't actually BELIEVE that you can have something, you will NOT attract it into your life.

Therefore, if you don't believe that you are sexy, funny, kind, confident, and WORTHY of a great man, you will not have a great man. Simple as that.

If I asked you, point-blank right now, what are your favorite things about yourself, what would you say?

Could you give me at least five things?!

Sadly, many women CANNOT.

It's time to step into your power, lovely, and see just how beautiful and amazing you truly are!

And for those of you who COULD rattle off five things you love about yourself, I'm going to up the game. Give me 30. And don't stop until you have the list complete!

The "30 Reasons" list is a tool I use with clients who could use a little boost in the self-love department. The premise is simple, instead of continually looking for reasons why you aren't good enough or aren't sexy enough or why life is not working out in your favor; instead you are going to look at all the ways you are lovely, you are amazing, and that everything is just great the way it is today.

When you shift your focus to the positive, it's as though you become a magnet for more positive events happening to you! What you focus upon grows. Just like giving a seed water, nutrients, and sunlight so that it can grow into the plant it was designed to become, giving yourself a daily reminder of your awesomeness will help you to grow and evolve into the shining human being you are meant to be!

Exercise: 30 Reasons I Am The Prize

Number your paper from 1 to 30.

For each number, write down one reason why you are the prize. It can be anything such as:

- I have a great butt.

- I am good with kids.

- I speak French.

You know you better than anyone else, and you are not allowed to stop until you have 30 things written on that little sheet of paper.

Now the fun part, read it back to yourself out loud!

Read it in the morning before you go to work. Read it before a date. Read it before you go to the movies.

The goal is to remind yourself constantly what a great catch you are. I promise it will raise your vibration and your sparkle and shift your point of attraction, so not only do you start to attract higher quality people into your life, but you'll continuously feel better about yourself.

And that, my dear, truly is the point behind everything that we are doing together.

CLIENT SUCCESS STORY: My client Alana suffered from low self-confidence. She'd been engaged and broke it off with a drug-addict who abused her. She needed some serious shifts in how she perceived herself. She completed this exercise and read her list daily for 30 days before going out in the morning. Guess what happened after a month!? She called me and left me this voicemail: *Emyrald! I've met the man of my dreams. I can't wait for you to meet him!*

Raise your vibration. Increase the quality of men you meet.

Fill in the blank:
I love myself because _____.

Day 7
Free Day!

"In order to love who you are, you cannot hate the experiences that shaped you."
—Andrea Dykstra

Wow. You've done a lot this week. I encourage you to read through your journal and see the desires of your heart on paper. How does it feel in your body to finally acknowledge what it is that you want and finally give yourself permission to have it?

I don't know about you, but there were too many wasted years of my life where I thought what I wanted was wrong, shameful, or simply not right.

Now I live from my heart.

If my heart truly desires something, I give it all I've got to make sure I experience it. I am worthy of experiencing massive abundance and prosperity on a material and spiritual level (and so are you!).

I love my whole self freely. There are no parts of me that I'm ashamed of any longer.

I am deserving of having all that my heart desires, and so are you, dear one.

Today I want you to do something for you. What does your heart desire today? How can you put down all the shoulds and instead embrace your desires?

Everything you want is perfect. It's time to start being more selfish and put yourself first. You are the most important person in your life because you are the person you are going to live with for the rest of your life.

Understood!?

Talk to you tomorrow!

Week 3

THE EVIL STEPMOTHER

"We accept the love we think we deserve"
—Stephen Chbosky

D id you ever see the movie, *The Perks of Being a Wallflower?* In it, the main character says the brilliant quote above in response to his love life not working out as planned.

So many kind and loving men waste years of their lives chasing after bitchy women who don't value or respect them.

And so many really nice women give up on the entire male population because of one or two jerks they dated.

Even more so, many people stay in unhealthy and toxic relationships! Why?

Because we accept the love we think we deserve.

Right now there is an Evil Stepmother in your head telling you things like:

- "No, you can't. You'll never get the job, so don't even apply."
- "You're too stupid to be loved. You'll always be alone. So don't even bother going on that dating site."
- "You're not good enough."
- "You'll never be as pretty as those girls, so why even try?"

This week is all about identifying your own personal Evil Stepmother (a.k.a. your limiting beliefs), removing them, and replacing them with your new way of being (a.k.a. the strong, confident Princess who knows what she wants and goes out and gets it!)

Depending on how you were raised and WHO you were raised by, you are going to have your own personal cocktail of limiting beliefs that are intoxicating at best and wreak havoc on your life at worst.

Once we dig deeper into what your Evil Stepmother says, you'll actually start to hear a very clear voice, and it will sound like your mother, your father, your grandparents, your siblings, the media, or that mean kid from 2nd grade who told you that you were fat.

The Evil Stepmother isn't real.

She's a figment of your imagination, and the longer you continue to believe what this made-up person says, the longer you will continue to struggle in the love department. And also in the money, job, career, and happiness departments as well.

I want you to decide NOW that it is time to stop paying that bitch's rent in your mind-space.

You CAN make that conscious decision today to stop believing what she says, and this week you'll learn how to do that, plus, you will learn who to listen to instead.*

*Hint - It's your Fairy Godmother.

Day 1

The Evil Stepmother

Cinderella: *[enters stepmother's bedroom after Gus is found under a teacup] Oh, please, you don't think that I would...*

Stepmother: *[interrupting] Hold your tongue! Now, it seems we have time on our hands.*

Cinderella: *But, I was only trying to...*

Stepmother: *[interrupting] Silence! Time for vicious practical jokes. Perhaps we can put it to better use. Now, let me see... There's the large carpet in the main hall- Clean it! And the windows upstairs and down- Wash them! Oh yes, and the tapestries and the draperies...*

Cinderella: *[interrupting] But I just finished...*

Stepmother: *[interrupting] Do them again! And don't forget the garden. Then scrub the terrace, sweep the halls and the stairs, clean the chimneys. And, of course, there's the mending, and the sewing, and the laundry... Oh, yes, and one more thing: see that Lucifer gets his bath.*

Have you ever heard of certain expressions or words such as limiting beliefs, the ego, egotistical thoughts, the monkey mind, your fears, fearful thoughts, and the inner child?

In my mind, you can lump all of these words into one overriding principle that wreaks havoc on your life: the Evil Stepmother.

The Evil Stepmother is a voice inside of your head that is holding you back from love. She's holding you back from greatness; she's holding you back from the fullest expression of YOU that is possible.

Every single person has an Evil Stepmother, and what she says is going to be different for us all depending on how you were raised and what 'issues' you need to get over in this lifetime.

Some people have an issue making money. Some always date the same dead-end losers. Some will always be taken advantage of. Yet others seem to have issues losing: losing money, losing love, losing precious items, etc.

Because of your own life experience, you will form a set of belief systems.

A belief system is neither right nor wrong. It is merely a combination of thoughts that you have thought enough times that they have planted seeds and taken root deep within your consciousness and now... they are a set of overriding principles as to HOW you live your life and WHAT you've come to expect.

Imagine, if you will, that you are driving a car down a road. YOU are the one who is behind the wheel and so YOU are the one who can keep the car on the road or go out of control and swerve off of the road. The car does not turn to the right when the road sharply banks to the right. The car waits for your direction. If you continue to go straight, the car will go off of the road into a ditch.

Was that wrong?

Is it the car's fault that it's now broken down on the side of the road?

Of course not! It was merely taking directions from the driver.

The same is true for the thoughts in your mind that become your belief system. Your body and mind are merely taking directions from you.

You're not good enough to get that promotion, you say? *Check! Keeping you right at the income level you're at, right away, ma'am!*

There are no good men in your town? *Got it. Allowing you only to see the ones that are losers and abusers.*

Are you not good enough or worthy of love? *Ok, why don't we keep those extra 10 pounds so that you don't even have to worry about dating or having your heart broken again?*

There is nothing right or wrong behind what you think. YOU are the one steering the car down the path of your own life. This means that you have massive responsibility in creating the life you want...and it all starts with the thoughts that are inside your head.

You created the Evil Stepmother. The good news is that she can also be uncreated by you. You actually have the power to create a Fairy Godmother to listen to instead!

How does that sound?

Let's pretend you notice a cute guy from across the room while you're at a party. You nudge the two girlfriends standing next to you and say: Don't look now. Cutie at two o'clock, and he's totally checking me out!

Girlfriend One says: Oh girl, I've heard he's a total player and that he only dates models. Don't even waste your time.

Girlfriend Two says: Oooh, he is cute. Smile at him and wink. You never know!

Which girl do you listen to? Is one right? Is the other wrong? Or are they simply reflections of individual belief systems?

Too often throughout your day, I would wager a guess that you are listening to Girlfriend One way too much! Why else are you still single and stumbling over love?

It's time to listen to Girlfriend Two...aka your Fairy Godmother, who is consistently encouraging you and reminding you of your greatness!

Exercise: The Evil Stepmother vs. The Fairy Godmother

I want you to pretend that you are a small child of around five. And you've got the most horrible stepmother in the entire world. She screams and yells at you and tells you how wretched you are. Embody your inner Cinderella. What is that Evil Stepmother shouting?

Freely write all of these nasty things in your journal.

Then...

Split a sheet of paper down the middle with a line and write down everything the Evil Stepmother says on the left-hand side of the paper.

Once you have completed the task, on the right-hand side of the paper, you're going to write what the Fairy Godmother would say instead to comfort a small child who is crying.

For example:

Evil Stepmother: You're too stupid to get the job, so don't even bother applying.

Fairy Godmother: You can do anything you put your mind to! Apply yourself, apply for the job, and if it's meant to be, it will happen. If not, then something grander will come along!

Evil Stepmother: You're fat and ugly.

Fairy Godmother: You are beautiful and perfect exactly as you are!

Once you are done flipping the Evil Stepmother's sayings around on their head into what the Fairy Godmother would say instead, I want you to circle the top three that really resonate with you right now. What are the three messages and words of encouragement that you need to hear every single day?

Take those three and write them on a fresh sheet of paper and post it somewhere in your house (or car) where you can see your reminder messages of love every day and read it out loud and remind yourself of your greatness!

Make sure to read aloud your new power mantras (aka magic spells) at least once a day for the rest of the week!

Fill in the blank:

I'm so grateful for myself and my life because _____.

Day 2

Worrying Is Like
A Rocking Chair

"Worrying is like sitting on a rocking chair.
You don't get anywhere, but it gives you
something to do."
—English proverb

Have you ever found yourself worrying?
Of course, you have!
We worry about getting in car accidents, or planes falling out of the sky, or losing our jobs, or not having enough money, or our kids getting hit by buses, or a meteor crashing into the earth and ending life as we know it!

Everyone … everywhere, has worried about something at some point in their lives.

Unfortunately, many people spend MOST of their lives worrying about potential future events that may or may not happen.

Worrying is like praying for what you don't want.

Yet, it's so addictive to do so. We land the job of our dreams and then worry about losing the job. We finally find the man of our dreams and then worry about doing something to mess it up.

Worry. Worry. Worry.

Why? What good does it actually do? In some cases, I could see how it would be a prudent idea to look at the situation from all angles and be prepared for all probable scenarios.

For example, if you're taking a 3-month trek through the Amazon in Ecuador, you are going to think about all the potential situations that could happen and what you would need to be prepared. You'll pack certain ointments and items in the first aid kit in case someone gets bitten by a poisonous creature or you fall and break your ankle. You'll pack rain gear and bug spray. I would imagine you'd probably brush up on your Spanish while you're at it, too.

But, do you worry, every day leading up to the trip, about being bitten by an anaconda or falling off a cliff?

Some of us WOULD worry every single day about what COULD GO WRONG during the course of the trip.

Others would simply prepare for the worst-case scenario but then go about their day being EXCITED about the journey.

Life is your long, strange trip. Now you can choose to worry about everything or be excited about what's coming. I say let's focus our attention on WHAT'S NEXT!

When I first started my love coaching career, my ex and I went through some challenging months. There were plenty of times that we had conversations about our future and if it would be more aligned to split up and continue our paths separately.

I had massive FEAR, WORRY, and ANXIETY about our separation.

What would it mean for my business? Would anyone still hire a single love coach? Would I be a failure? Would I have to start all over again? What would I tell my tribe?

The list of fears went on and on and on.

Consequently, I sat myself down one day after I realized the worrying HAD to stop and played a little game called: What's the worst that could happen?

Here's how you play the game:

You take one of your fears. In my case, the fear of splitting from my man and what that would mean for the future of my business.

You then trace the fear down to the very end of the rope by asking yourself, '*And then what?*' after every logical conclusion.

So in my example:

I'm worried that if my man and I break up, then it would harm my business.

And then what?

I'd lose any traction I built, lose my clients, become broke, and have to start over again.

And then what?

What would I tell my clients and mailing list? Am I a failure in their eyes?

And then what?

Well, I would explain that even though you love someone and even though you're soulmates, it does not guarantee that you're meant to spend the rest of your life together.

And then what?

Well, I might lose some clients because they don't think I can truly help them out because now I'm single.

And then what?

Or, I might also gain some clients who are in a relationship having the same fears and concerns themselves, and I'll be an inspiration to them.

And then what?

I'd be true to myself, speaking my truth, and there are plenty of people out there who need to learn how to consciously end a relationship regardless of how much love there is between the two people.

And then what?

I'd simply have a new direction for my business based around following one's heart and being able to step out of a relationship that is not 100% in alignment with what the heart wants...which is precisely what I teach my clients. And it's exactly what happened. My ex and I *did* split up. And I was able to teach from a deep place of integrity about leaving (versus staying in) a relationship that was no longer in alignment. And the end result being: a relationship that is 100% in alignment with myself and my higher purpose on the planet.

Do NOT settle. You can have it all.

By playing the "What's The Worst That Could Happen" game, it actually traces the root of your fear down to the end, and it ends up with a resolution quite quickly. I did the same thing when I was worrying about money and finances. I transmuted the fear and worry of, "What if I don't get enough clients this month to pay my bills and pay off my debt" to, "so then you get another job while you are building your coaching practice so that you have the safety net to pay off your obligations."

Don't allow your fears to control you. Once you face them head-on, you have power over them. You'll realize that they aren't so scary after all.

Remember that scene in *Home Alone* with Macaulay Culkin, where he's scared to go down into the basement because the radiator makes weird noises? He sees it light up, and he repeats his positive affirmation: *It's only my imagination. It's only my imagination.*

But it doesn't work. The radiator starts laughing menacingly, and he runs upstairs, screaming!

But by the end of the movie and after a lot of growing up, he goes downstairs and faces that radiator head-on saying something along the lines of *"Hey, I'm not afraid anymore. I said I'm not afraid anymore. Do you hear me? I'm not afraid anymore!"*

Ok, if you're familiar with the movie, that's actually slightly out of order, but you get the point here.

By the end of the movie, he DOES realize that the radiator is just a radiator, and it is nothing to be frightened of. But it took him a while to get to that point.

Exercise: What's The Worst That Could Happen?

Write down five of your biggest fears in your journal.

Pick one that scares you the most and trace it down to the end using questions like:

And then what?

And then what happens?

Once you reach a conclusion, you'll realize your fears aren't so scary after all. We tend to make them worse in our minds because we don't face them logically. In fact, we rarely face them at all! We simply push them aside with a fearful "I don't want to think about that!"

Congrats! You just took a giant step towards becoming FEARLESS!

Fill in the blank:
I'm so grateful for myself and my life because _____.

Day 3

Quit Shoulding Yourself

> "Should is shit, so quit
> 'shoulding' yourself."
> ## - My Dad, James Schumacher

Our "shoulds" hold us back from what we really want to do. It's not being true to who you really are. Should is just as debilitating as those limiting beliefs holding you back. Instead of pursuing a lifelong dream of being a singer, you went to school and studied accounting because it's the 'safe' route, and your parents thought you should do it.

Or, all you really wanted was to be a stay at home dad who focused on gardening, but you went to business school because you 'should' do the responsible thing.

Today we are going to unravel what is going on underneath the surface of what is getting in the way of having the love of your life and the life of your dreams.

I should... be a good person.

I should... get a stable job.

I shouldn't... sell all my belongings and travel the world.

Instead, if you were doing the exact thing you LOVED to be doing and your days were filled with joy, you would most likely be an inspiration to those around you!!

Let's say you were from a small town in Illinois (like myself). All you really want to do is travel the world.

And yet, as soon as you graduate from high school, you go to college and get your business degree. Why?

Because it was what I 'should' do. But as soon as I could, I traveled abroad and studied in Spain. And then I came back to the US and graduated. Now what? What *should* I do? Should I get a job and pay off my debt? That's the logical conclusion.

Luckily for me, I realized at that point in my life that wasn't what I 'wanted' to do. Even though it was what I 'should' do. So I followed my heart, moved to Ecuador, and traveled South America for close to 10 years. Those 10 years taught me so much about life and the world. I grew spiritually, culturally, and lived more in those 10 years than many live in their entire lives! Screw those student loans.

It was my passion and what I wanted to do. Regardless of what the Midwesterners thought I 'should' do.

Now, I'm not saying to be irresponsible and ignore your debt. The point of the story is to follow your heart and not listen to the 'shoulds' that live in and around you.

Exercise: The Should Exercise

Step One: Write down all the things you 'should' be doing in your life.

Example:

I should be making more money.

I should grow my own food.

I should get a better job.

I should be a better mother.

Step Two: Rewrite that list but instead start it with "I could."

I could be making more money.

I could grow my own food.

I could get a better job.

I could be a better mother.

These shoulds weigh you down. But when you shift it to "I could," can you feel the energetic difference here? All of a sudden, you are given a choice to create what you want in your life instead of what you HAVE to do.

Step Three: Rewrite the second list with only the items that you WANT to do.

I want to make more money.

I want to grow my own food.

I want to get a better job.

I want to be a better mother.

This gets you away from all the ideas in your head of what you should do based on your parents or friends or society.

Exceptions - Maybe you have a job, and you cannot really say that you 'want' to get to work on time because you'd rather be sleeping in. So why not rephrase it as "I choose to arrive to work on time." This puts the power of choice in your life. You are no longer the victim. You choose to get to work on time because you desire to keep your job and continue to make the money you are making. Ultimately you do not have to go to work on time, but you choose to.

Instead of looking at all of your obligations as 'shoulds' weighing you down, this simple act of rephrasing your words and thoughts brings more joy into your life because of the power of choice that you always have!

Today I invite you to really look closely at your life and make sure your actions are in alignment with what you want and what you choose.

When you catch yourself shoulding all over yourself, what you do to get yourself out of it, is to become aware. You have to be your own observer and catch yourself. You have to be the one who decides that you want to change. And then you have to be the one to create said change.

Your challenge should you choose to accept it: Remove the word SHOULD from your vocabulary immediately!

Fill in the blank:
I'm so grateful for myself and my life because _____.

Day 4

Burn Baby, Burn!

"Some of us think holding on makes us
strong, but sometimes it is letting go."

—Herman Hesse

Have you ever done anything you were NOT proud of?
Ugh, I have.
In college, I was a bit lost. I was looking for love in all of the
wrong places. I told you a bit in my "Love Story" earlier. I was looking
externally for love instead of searching within.

I'm not proud to admit that I used sex (unsuccessfully) for love.
I thought it would get me MORE love, when instead it ended up
in getting less. I felt like crap. I was ashamed of myself for sleeping
around. And ultimately, I felt low, low, low amounts of love for myself
because nobody else loved me.

I remember one night in Mexico, sleeping with a married man.
He was older and attractive, and I was drunk on tequila. He was more
than flattered that a 21-year-old was interested in him, and we went
back to his art studio.

Returning home to where I was staying that night, something was bothering me in the back of my mind. I tried to push it out. I tried to ignore it.

The next morning when I woke up, I went to the plaza mayor with the other women in the study abroad program. I drank freshly squeezed juices (that they are selling on almost every corner) to push the night and my uneasy feelings out of my mind.

Something was still bothering me, but what?

I looked across the plaza and - gasp!

What did I see?

Or more accurately, *who* did I see?

The married man. Smiling and walking across the plaza with his arm around his wife.

I swear to you, I think he looked back over his shoulder and saw me staring at the two of them.

And a weight sank deep into my stomach.

THAT is why I felt like shit. My consciousness knew that what I had done was not in alignment with who I really was.

I was not in alignment with my actions, and that is why I felt the way I did. And life has a poetic way of slapping you in the face sometimes.

It was as though the great cosmic hand in the sky was wagging its finger at me while saying 'tsk, tsk, tsk' under its breath.

I knew that I was better than my actions. I believed in fidelity and honesty between partners. I also knew I wanted so much more than to be some man's mistress for a night while in Mexico.

When I returned to the US after that semester abroad, the uneasy feeling continued to nag at me. HOW could I let go of what had happened and start over again? If such a thing was possible?

Without going into all of the details, I was talking to my boss about how I was feeling. I didn't tell her exactly what had happened but simply that there were some things in my life that I was not proud of and wanted to let go of and move on from.

She suggested the exercise that I lay out for you below.

I went back to my room immediately and did the exercise. I still remember the feeling of release I felt as I watched the paper burn.

Today, it's still an exercise I use for letting go. Fire is a potent substance, allowing you to transform something (a piece of paper, for example) from one energetic state into another.

When you burn the paper, you symbolically let that shit go! Transmute and shift the energy from one state to another! Everything that has happened in your life is there for a reason. It has brought you to where you are today. It's time to change your energy around it. If you don't move through past and current lessons, you are bound to repeat them over and over and over again.

So, if you have stuff from your past that weighs you down, the best way to move on is to face it head-on and then consciously let that situation go energetically.

Exercise: Burn, Baby, Burn!

Write down everything in your life that you are ashamed of. Things that you are not proud of. Things that weigh you down. Write it all down on a sheet (or more) of paper.

Then go outside to a safe place and BURN that sheet of paper.

After the paper has burned, say the following out loud:

I thank you, shadow side, for all the lessons you have given me. You've brought me to this moment in time, and I now choose, out of love and compassion for myself, to LET THIS ALL GO.

Fill in the blank:

I'm so grateful for myself and my life because _____.

Day 5

Hello, I'm Perfect.
Nice To Meet You.

"One of the deepest habitual patterns
that we have is the feeling that the present
moment is not enough."
—Pema Chodron

Don't you ever get tired of not being happy where you are? Doesn't it ever get old wishing for more than you presently have? Aren't you sick and tired of abusing your body and hoping that it will somehow magically change because you wish it were so?

For the longest time (around 28 years), I always believed that I was flawed. If only I could lose 10 pounds around my stomach, then I would be perfect.

If only my skin would clear up, then I would be beautiful.

If only I could make more money, then I would be happy.

This pattern continued for way too many years. Until one day I read something by Pema Chodron that changed it all for me:

"There is a story of a woman running away from tigers. She runs and runs, and the tigers are getting closer and closer. When she comes to the edge of a cliff, she sees some vines there, so she climbs down and holds onto the vines.

Looking down, she sees that there are tigers below her as well. She then notices that a mouse is gnawing away at the vine to which she is clinging. She also sees a beautiful little bunch of strawberries close to her, growing out of a clump of grass. She looks up, and she looks down. She looks at the mouse. Then she just takes a strawberry, puts it in her mouth, and enjoys it thoroughly.

Tigers above, tigers below. This is actually the predicament that we are always in, in terms of our birth and death. Each moment is just what it is.

It might be the only moment of our life; it might be the only strawberry we'll ever eat. We could get depressed about it, or we could finally appreciate it and delight in the preciousness of every single moment of our life."

I got chills when I read that passage, and it sunk in as I realized how much of my life I had been wasting wishing for something that simply was not what I had.

From that day forward, I vowed to myself that I would focus on the beauty and the perfection in every single moment, instead of the microscopic focus of everything that I did NOT want in my life.

I got off the couch and went to the mirror, and I just looked at my body, and for the first time ever, I appreciated and enjoyed it. I ran my hands up and down my body and said things like: You are perfect. You are beautiful. I love you. Thank you.

Something shifted in my mind, and I understood the privilege it was simply to be in my body! And not only that, to have strong legs for working out. And to have a healthy stomach that could digest food with ease. And to have sensitive skin that would alert me (via a breakout) if I were eating foods that my body did not agree with.

I'm not able to magically pass that aha moment onto you so that all your insecurities and body-bashing go away. But I can offer you the suggestion that perhaps you are perfect. Maybe every single thing that has happened to you (no matter how horrible it might seem at first) actually was divinely orchestrated to bring you to where you are today.

> "The place where you are right now,
> God circled on a map for you."
> **—Hafiz**

For the next day, I'd like you to embrace the radical possibility that everything (yes - everything!) is perfect. Your house is perfect. Your car is perfect. Your body is perfect. Your crazy loud neighbor is perfect. Your food allergies are perfect. Every single thing you can point the finger at or direct your attention to is 100% perfect because it's all playing a part in your life.

Contrast is playing the role of showing you what you want and do NOT want at any given moment. If not for experiencing the shame and pain of sleeping with a married man, I wouldn't have had the awakening of what I did want in a relationship: a man deeply committed to me and our spiritual growth together.

Contrast is experiencing the light alongside the dark. If not for the darkness, you would not be able to appreciate the light.

If not for being betrayed and cheated upon, how could you truly grow in learning how to set boundaries and stand up for yourself?

If not for disrespecting yourself and setting firm boundaries in one relationship, how could you become stronger and experience a closer and more powerful relationship in the future?

Everything that has happened in your life has given you the opportunity to grow, evolve, and shine into the beautiful human being that you are today.

I'd like to leave you with an anonymous poem (that I've adapted and changed slightly) that I read in many of my yoga classes because I do feel it drives this point home.

I asked for strength and was given difficulties to make me strong.
I asked for wisdom and was given problems to solve.
I asked for prosperity and was given brawn and brains to work.
I asked for courage and was given dangers to overcome.
I asked for patience and was placed in situations where I was forced to wait.
I asked for love and was given troubled people to help.
I asked for favors and was given opportunities, instead.
I asked for everything I wanted so I could enjoy life.
Instead, I was given life so I could enjoy everything.
I received nothing I wanted, but received everything I needed to grow and evolve into the shining human being I am meant to be!

Exercise: What If Everything Were Perfect?

In your journal, reflect upon the following questions:

1. What if all parts of you were perfect?

2. In what ways has your shadow side led to the life you have today and massive growth/change?

3. What if EVERYTHING that happened in your life (including your limiting beliefs and the Evil Stepmother in your head) was for a reason?

Fill in the blank:
I'm so grateful for myself and my life because _____.

Day 6

The Fairy Godmother Speaks!

"It's not what you look at that matters, it's what you see."

—Henry David Thoreau

Today we conclude week three by installing new beliefs into your consciousness. Whoop whoop!!

The beliefs that we hold create our life.

How?

Let's say you are 10 years old and you've just given a presentation in front of your class. When complete, your teacher praises you and says you've done an excellent job and that you're a fantastic speaker and that she really is impressed at how well you've done. "You are years ahead of most," she exclaims happily to you.

From that moment onward, you decide that you are an excellent speaker. You take public speaking classes in high school. You become a master debater in college. And ultimately, you grow up to be a public speaker inspiring the masses to change!

Now let's say you were a different 10-year-old in the same class and you're really nervous about getting in front of a class and speaking because at home you have two older brothers and you never get a word in. You've developed a slight stutter because of your fear of being noticed, and you never have the opportunity to be the center of attention, and you're intimidated as to how it will go.

Because of your fears, you stutter over many of your words, accidentally skip over some crucial points, and ultimately mess-up your presentation.

Instead of saying, "That's OK, great job," the teacher focuses on all the ways you messed up and where you could improve your speech. After a couple of minutes of what she perceives as helpful pointers, she concludes by saying, "Some people just aren't good at speaking on stage."

From that moment onward, you decide NEVER to speak again in front of a large group of people. Later on in life, you are skipped over for promotions because you never take credit for your ideas and allow them to go to the outspoken man in the group project. You suffer from low self-confidence and spend most of your free time alone, nose in a book. You've decided long ago that you're not really smart, that you're not a good speaker, so why really try and put yourself out there?

For you, life is comfortable. You exist. But you NEVER put yourself out there.

We can internalize a belief system immediately, or it can happen slowly over time. Your father can yell at you once and tell you, "you'll never amount to anything," and you decide that it's true and grow up with the belief that you are flawed and stupid.

Or, your father can tell you every single day how stupid you are and how worthless you are, and after many years of hearing it, you finally decide it's true.

This works for the positive as well.

I was always encouraged to follow my heart growing up. My parents would read me inspirational books such as, "Oh, The Places You'll Go!" by Dr. Seuss. And I believe it's a big part of why I'm so independent with a thirst for travel!

So how do you go about actually changing the underlying belief systems that you have?

We've already done a couple of exercises to get you started! Flip back to the statements that the "Fairy Godmother" told you in day one of this week. That's your start right there! Intuitively you already know what you need to hear to start to shift your belief systems.

We come from one source of love if I may say so myself. Some call it God. Some say The Universe. I simply call it Love.

Inside of your body and heart, you know your true source.

But your silly belief systems are getting in the way of you experiencing it!

Let's harness the power of your imagination a little bit more, shall we?

Who is the person you truly desire to be? Do you wish to be with a partner who adores you and cherishes you and you laugh for hours on end with? Do you want to be confident and feel sexy and speak what is on your mind?

If you desire to make $20,000 a month with your jewelry business but are presently making $4,000 a month, what would it take to be that woman who is making $20k? I guarantee there are plenty of people making a lot of money in their jewelry businesses. One of my dear friends makes close to $250,000 a year with her jewelry business!! So, with that being the case, what are the belief systems that she probably has?

I would guess things like:

Making money is easy for me.
There are so many shops that want to buy my jewelry.
There is always a waiting list for my products.
I love sales and am great at selling!

Can you think of more beliefs that a woman with a 6-figure jewelry business would have?

One of the most significant differences between a $4k a month business and a $20,000 a month business is the BELIEF that it is possible. And yes, some knowledge, hard work, and big breaks will make a difference too.

I can also tell you that if you do not believe something is possible, you will not take the action steps towards it.

If you don't believe you'll get the job, you won't apply.

If you don't believe she'll say yes, you won't ask her out.

So, how do you change those pesky beliefs that are getting in your way?

Well, you use your imagination and pretend you are that person who BELIEVES a different way.

And then, you follow this process.

Exercise: Future Me Belief Systems

1. Put on a song that puts you in a good mood. A song that makes you wanna dance. Put that song on LOUD and dance your face off! This gets those endorphins up!

2. Then make a list of all those beliefs that a person who has what you desire would believe.

3. Read that list out loud.

4. Repeat daily.

To really blow your mind, read those beliefs out loud into a recording device, and then play it back to yourself. Do you actually believe yourself? If not, read them out loud again and play it back. Keep doing it until YOU actually believe what it is, you just said.

THAT is when you are starting to change the belief systems your body has.

A question I hear a lot: *Why do we have to put on music first and dance?*

Because emotion is energy in motion! *E-Motion.*

It's essential to put on music that gets your energy levels up and your vibration high! This gets you in a positive feeling state. From there, when you say your new beliefs, your body is actually in the state to receive these new belief systems. If you're simply going through the motions and stating I AM BEAUTIFUL. I LOVE MYSELF. I'M WORTHY OF MAKING $20,000 A MONTH, but there is no emotion behind what you are saying, nothing will move.

E-motion = energy in motion.

You've got to get those energy levels UP for your new belief systems to hold on tight.

Got it?

Do this exercise every single day. THIS is how you change your belief systems.

Disclaimer: They say it takes anywhere from 90 to 365 days to create new neural pathways in your brain. That means if you've been thinking a thought your entire life and created a belief system around it, it is going to take anywhere from 3 months to a year of doing this exact process to actually retrain your brain to think a different way and to respond differently to your thoughts and integrate a new belief system.

Yes, you can create a brand new you. And yes, it will take some time and consistent effort.

But let's be real, for a moment. Isn't it worth it? Eye on the prize, love. You got this!

Fill in the blank:
I'm so grateful for myself and my life because _____.

Day 7

The Attitude
Of Gratitude

"Gratitude turns what
we have into enough."

—Aesop

On your day off today, I'd like you to bask in a state of Gratitude. What does that mean?

It merely means being grateful for every person and experience that steps into your life.

Adopt an attitude of gratitude.

That's it. Appreciate and be grateful for all the people in your life and all the experiences that brought you to where you are today. Be grateful to be alive. Be grateful to be in a body. Be grateful to be you.

And most importantly, love yo' self like you're all you've got, baby!

Week 4

WHEN YOU WISH UPON A STAR...

"When you wish upon a star, makes no difference who you are, your dreams will come true!"
- Jiminy Cricket in Pinocchio

re you ready to truly get honest with the desires in your heart? Are you prepared to put pen to paper and tell the Universe exactly what you want for your own personal Prince Charming? This week is when you'll wish upon a star and learn the proven tools to help you bring Prince Charming one (or one-hundred) steps closer to you!

Now, I'm also not naive enough to tell you that if you just close your eyes real hard and wish, wish, wish, that when you open them a smart, handsome billionaire with a 7-carat engagement ring is going to be down on one knee in front of you (more on that in week five actually).

But...

You must actually KNOW what you want in order to get it.

Imagine this:

Your Great Aunt Lorie asks you what you want for your birthday, and you reply, "Oh, anything is fine by me!"

Guess what you actually get for your birthday?

Well - it could be anything. It could be something you love (like a new Kate Spade purse), it could be something that is just ok (like a gift card to Barnes and Nobles), or it could be absolutely dreadful (like that one time she got you a sweater with the owls on it).

The point I'm trying to make here is that unless you make your desires known, you are very, very, very unlikely to get what you want.

And not only that, many women have no idea what they want. Women are so used to going with the crowd and putting themselves last that when I pointedly ask a woman what she wants in her life, she has no idea.

Now is the time to get clear on what you do want in a man. Please do NOT hold back. I've gotten EVERYTHING I've wanted on my list down to the size of his...heart. And he's got a big one!

If I can make this clear just one more time:

When you tell Aunt Lorie that you'd like the entire series collection of *Sex and the City* plus movies 1 and 2, and precisely the link on Amazon to purchase the boxed set at 77% off, you are about 99.99% likely to get precisely what you want. An added bonus is you have the evenings of the next couple of months planned out with glasses of wine and your BFFs Carrie, Samantha, Miranda and Charlotte to keep you company.

See where I'm going here?

Let's go about getting you what you want, girl!

The exercises this week are going to build on one another, every day is adding to the day before. We are going to BUILD a personal daily routine that is extremely powerful in attracting your Prince to you!

Don't take the exercises lightly. Magic will happen, my dear!

Day 1

Prince Charming

"True, that he's no Prince Charming, but there's something in him that I simply didn't see before."
—Beauty from Beauty and the Beast

Ready to put your Perfect Prince Charming order in with the Universe?

Of course, you are! That's why you're here, isn't it?

Before we do that, I have to share with you why so many women have it backward when it comes to dating and men.

Trisha always found herself dating the same type of man. He was egotistical, self-centered, and ultimately she ended it because he cheated on her.

But her priorities were all wrong when she was on a first date. She'd look for the superficial qualities in a man such as if he was handsome and how much money he made.

Those items right there are what I refer to as 'Icing on the Cake.' It's absolutely perfect to want to be with a man who is easy on the eyes and makes good money. But those are not the qualities you look for *first* in a partner. When you stay with a man because he's cute and then work on getting to know him, what I find happens to most women is that they become intimate, have sex, and consequently fall in love with a man who is entirely wrong for them!

If only she knew how to organize her priorities so that she wouldn't go down the path with a man who really doesn't deserve a second date with her!

That is why I've created a three-part list to help you get clear on what you want in a partner and also how to rate those priorities.

By using this process, it will not only help you weed out those who are not a good fit for you, but you're also putting your order into the Universe of just precisely what it is you desire in a partner.

Once Trisha and I organized her Prince Charming into three lists, she was able to see that she was doing things backward, and that is why she kept ending up with the same wrong man for her. Once she switched things around, she actually found a really nice man that she's now dating. He opens doors for her. He pays attention to her needs and feelings. And ultimately, she feels cherished when she is around him. Her personal transformation resulted in a complete 180-degree turn!

 Exercise: Create Your Personal Prince Charming List

The point in today's exercise is not only to get clear in what you want but also to prioritize those traits in your perfect man so you don't get caught up in what doesn't really matter. Because let's be real, if a man treats you exactly how you want to be treated, you feel loved around him, you talk until the early hours of the morning about topics that matter to you, and you laugh with him unlike anyone else you've laughed with, I'd wager a bet that you really wouldn't care if he had a little potbelly or wasn't as tall as you thought your perfect man would be.

It's all about ordering your priorities, and plenty of the items on the 'Icing on the Cake' list don't really matter when a man fulfills your "Non-Negotiables" and your "Heart's Desire" lists.

Here's what you need to do:

On the first sheet of paper, title it NON-NEGOTIABLES

On this paper, you'll write items that are so important to you that this person would not make it to a second date. For example, if you know that you want kids, 'wants kids' would be on that list. If you're not sure yet about kids, 'open to the possibility of kids' would be on that list.

If your dad was an alcoholic and you're a strict non-drinker, and that's really important to you that your partner does not drink, that should be on your list.

If you're a health nut and cannot stand the smell of cigarettes, 'non-smoker' would be on that list.

Do you see where I'm going here?

This list really doesn't need to be that long. It's most likely going to be a short list. Unless you're really, really, really picky. In which case, who am I to judge? But you might want to reconsider what indeed is not negotiable and if you're just being too demanding.

When dating, do NOT go on a second date with someone who is not 100% of the list you just wrote above. You must find out on that first date if he/she passes the test, so to speak, and meets your non-negotiables and is worthy of a second date. Yes, look at it as an interview. Don't be scared to ask questions like, "What are your thoughts on marriage? Do you want to have kids? What's your biggest goal/dream in life?" If he cannot easily answer these questions, he is not emotionally mature and ready for a woman like you. Buh-bye.

If you are too scared to ask pointed questions like this as you're interviewing potential candidates to be your life partner, then YOU are not ready for a relationship of that caliber. In which case, do some personal growth work first and save dating for later.

On the second sheet of paper, title it HEART'S DESIRE.

The items on this list are going to be traits or qualities that you would like to share with your partner that would make life enjoyable. Think about the traits or qualities that you share with your friends. You're never 100% the same as your friends, but you have enough in common that you enjoy certain activities together.

When you're dating and 'interviewing' potential candidates for the role of taking care of your heart, I would suggest looking for a partner who is 70% or so of this list.

On the third sheet of paper, title it ICING ON THE CAKE.

This list is where you get to be completely superficial and fill it with items like tall, dark and handsome with his own personal airplane and a self-made millionaire.

I had a client write these things above on her list. And guess what? She got most of them!!

How's that for manifesting capabilities?

Once again, the point of this exercise is to help you get clear on what you want but to also recognize in a rational way what is truly important when you're interviewing life partners versus what is just icing on the cake.

CLIENT SUCCESS STORY:

My client Tracy said the following:

"I found myself settling for guys that were 'reasonable' and interested in me. I was willing to overlook lots of things that didn't feel quite right. In fact, I was not even noticing these things consciously because I wanted to be in a relationship more than I wanted the right relationship. I'm not even sure I knew what that right relationship would have looked like."

After I helped her get clear on the desires of her heart, she was able to filter her matches only to men that seemed to be a great fit based on her Prince Charming list. And all of a sudden, THESE men were really respecting the fact that she 'knew what she wanted.'

One man even told her that he was so impressed by her 'confidence.'

The end result? Tracy is now dating an amazing man, and she sent me this email a while back as an update:

"After working with you both in the course and in private coaching, I was able to really get in touch with myself and my relationship needs. Once this was clarified, I no longer tolerated the ill-fitting suitors. I was able to pass on them and not waste my time.

Honestly, working with Emyrald in our private 1:1 coaching on top of the group really solidified these concepts and gave me the confidence to demand so much more for myself. And it worked - by the end of the course, I had met a wonderful man who fit my needs and was equally into me.

Thanks, Emyrald, for helping me up my dating game to this level. It has forever changed me."

Complete the following sentence:

I deserve to have everything my heart desires because

_____.

Day 2

Follow Your Excitement

"Focus on the excitement and it will
lead you through the obstacles."

—Piya Sarcar

Think about a time in life when you were really excited because something amazing just happened.

What did you do?

Most likely, you called a girlfriend up and gushed to her about this incredible such and such that just occurred, right?

Your emotions were high, and you were feeling great, and you just HAD to share with another what just happened!

How do you think you would feel if the tremendous "I-just-met-the-love-of-my-life!" suddenly happened to you?

Chances are you'd do what my client Alisa did. She called me up immediately and left me a voicemail, gushing: "Oh my god, Emyrald! I just met the man of my dreams. I can't wait for you to meet him!"

What if you could reverse the chain of events and get just as excited about meeting 'the one' before you even met him?

Suppose that by pretending that the encounter of a lifetime already happened, you could create a chain of events that actually puts him in your path?

Too often we put ourselves unknowingly in a waiting place. Once we get the guy, then we'll be excited. A + B = C.

Instead, I'm suggesting that you immediately LEAP straight to the end-game: feeling excitement for the man of your dreams in your life so that the Universe can assemble all of the pieces into place that are necessary for him to actually manifest.

Doesn't that sound absolutely fabulous?

Today, I'm giving you a fantastic exercise that you can apply for just about anything in life that you want to create. (However, we'll get more into potions and spells next week.)

Exercise: Prince Charming Audio

Pull out your smartphone and open up the app to record an audio.

Pretend you are talking to a girlfriend, tell her all about this amazing man you just met, how wonderful he is, explain that he fits your list, and is even better than you could have imagined!

See my audio as an example.
(www.emyraldsinclaire.com/destinationsoulmate)

Conversely, if you can't record the audio, say it into the mirror every day instead!

Then, your homework is to listen to it as much as you can over the next week to keep yourself in that high vibration of excitement for this man that is coming into your life!

Complete the following sentence:
I deserve to have everything my heart desires because

_____.

Day 3

Get On The Train!

"Even if you're on the right track, you'll still get run over if you just sit there."

—Will Rogers

et's keep the high-vibration train going and build on the last two days!

After putting your order out to the universe in the form of the Prince Charming list, you can rest assured that he is on his way.

Before you think that your role in this particular exercise is completed, remember that we do have a little bit of refinement left to do.

Let's pretend that there are 1 million men on the planet that could fulfill the requirements of those lists that you've just created.

I want you to imagine you're out to eat, and you've ordered a curry from the kitchen.

Be mindful there are numerous types of curries. Did you want a Vindaloo, a Korma, a Bombay, a Kashmir, a Nihari, or something else to your liking? Did you want beef, chicken, tofu, or veggies? How about the level of spice in your dish? Come on now; I know you are a SPICY woman!

These are all refinements to your perfect curry. Your curry order could literally be a thousand different curry combinations considering that there are 100s of types of curry available. (yum)

Writing your Prince Charming list is not nearly enough. We're going to get really, truly specific and take your curry order down from the potential of thousands or even hundreds of thousands of potential combinations, and reduce it to a particular order including taste, texture and spiciness level!

Today you're going to write a Future Memory with the love of your life.

Why do I ask this of you, you may be wondering as you wander about?

Because it's oh-so-personal to how you want to feel when you're with this person.

There are plenty of men out there who are kind, generous, good with kids, close to their mothers, tall, dark, handsome, and making over 6 figures a year.

Can you imagine how different it feels if one of these men surprises you with roses and you hop into his private jet and fly away to the Eiffel Tower for a weekend, versus if he surprises you with a 6-pack of beer and you jump into his 4-Runner, and he takes you away to the mountains for the weekend?

You may draft the same 'description' of the man, but picture and consider how you would feel about each of these experiences. You exert and exude a completely different energy out into the Universe of what you desire.

When I first did this exercise, I imagined this:

I was teaching a yoga class, and my man was in the front row. We'd catch each other's eyes and smile. I give him a couple of extra adjustments just so that I could put my hands on his body and offer him some personalized attention. I'd catch him looking at my butt, and he'd smile. After class, he'd be talking to some of my students, singing my praises. I just felt comfortable with my man, and he was comfortable coming to my yoga class. There was a special bond and closeness there.

This 'future memory' says so much more than merely a partner who comes to my yoga class and checks out my butt.

It speaks of a spiritual and athletic man who takes pride in his body and mind. This is a portrait of a man who is willing to support me in something that means a lot to me. This image is also representative of a man who is ready to try new things and move himself outside of his comfort zone.

When I met my ex, guess what? He'd never been to a yoga class before! Now, did I immediately scratch him off the list? No! Of course not! Because he also had so many of those other qualities on my 'non-negotiables' and 'heart's desire' list.

As we continued dating and he got to know me, he wanted to learn more. So he came to my yoga class and got hooked! He wasn't necessarily into the 'spiritual' aspect... in the beginning. However, over time, he really came to resonate with my teachings and look forward to the meditative aspect of my classes.

Yes, one day, I looked over at him in the front row and caught him looking at my butt, and we exchanged a smile. I realized that my future vision had just come true. I had manifested a man who I felt a certain way with!

Exercise: Your Future Memory

Write down a future memory with your man. It doesn't have to be complicated, but it should be very personal and unique to you. Think of the curry analogy. What type of Future Memory would help you to feel excited with your man and filled with love?

Complete the following sentence:
I deserve to have everything my heart desires because _____

Day 4

Visualize It, Baby

"I would just visualize things coming to me. It would just make me feel better. Visualization works if you work hard. That's the thing. You can't just visualize and go eat a sandwich."

—Jim Carrey

Did you know that your brain cannot tell the difference between what it sees, remembers and imagines?

The exact same parts of the brain light up whether you are looking at a cute man walking outside your window, you close your eyes and remember the hot guy walking past your window, or you simply imagine a stud-muffin walking outside your house.

Not only that, I once read about a study where they tested three groups for muscle growth and performance.

Group 1 is asked to perform a specific exercise for an hour a day for 30 days.

Group 2 is asked to think about performing a specific exercise for an hour a day for 30 days.

Group 3 does nothing.

As I'm sure you can guess, Group 1 increases the muscle mass of that muscle group up to 50% on average.

Incredibly what you might not have guessed is that Group 2 increased their muscle mass around 32%!

Group 3 - nothing changed.

Many would ponder the mystery how is it that group 2 created actual physical changes within their body by merely visualizing themselves doing the exercises?

The answer is a topic for another book entirely.

For today, we'll use that as a powerful example of the ultimate power of visualization.

 Exercise: Visualize Your Future Memory

Review the Future Memory you wrote yesterday. Today I'd like you to set your phone timer for 2 minutes and simply bask in the feelings of this future memory.

Visualize in technicolor as many aspects of the Future Memory that you can. What are you wearing? What do you smell? How does he feel in your arms? What do you notice going on around you? What color are the flowers?

From this moment forward, your homework is to practice this technique for 2 minutes a day every day! Yes, your future memory can change in future days. The point of the exercise is the very personal feelings that arise because of specific visualizations.

Complete the following sentence:

I deserve to have everything my heart desires because

_____.

Day 5

Core Desired Feelings

"Your core desired feelings should sit
at the center of all your intentions."
—Danielle LaPorte

Danielle LaPorte teaches about *Core Desired Feelings*. To explain this: the heart of the philosophy is how you want to feel on any given day.

Feelings such as:

- Connected. Beautiful. Loving. Abundant. Strong.
- Spacious. Free. Creative. Grounded.
- Thriving. Courageous. Innovative.
- Flow. Ineffable. Intentional. Potent.
- Powerful. Thankful. Nourishment. Freedom.
- Illuminable. Affluent. Expansive. True.
- Vibrant. Content. Peaceful. Worthy.
- Empowering. Ablaze. Whimsical. Aglow.

These feelings are very personal to you based on your individual constitution. As a result of the exercise yesterday, you were put in a particular emotional state.

Describe those precise emotions and sentiments.

Write them down NOW in your journal.

 ## Exercise: Core Desired Feelings

After you wrote down your *Core Desired Feelings* of how you'd like to feel within your relationship, review your list of feelings. Circle the Top 5 that are most important to you.

Now here's the fun part. Instead of waiting for a relationship to help you experience those feelings in the future, the goal is to fill your life with activities today so that you are experiencing those feelings now.

Transfer those top 5 feelings that are most important to you to a new sheet of paper. Brainstorm different activities that help you feel that way.

For example, one of my Core Desired feelings is Freedom. Activities that help me to feel free include travel, being financially solvent, exploring new places, and speaking my mind.

Consequently, I continually look for ways that I can feel free daily. I'll plan multiple trips per year, both alone and with my partner. I'm continuously searching for strategies to increase my income and decrease my debt (or stay debt-free!). I am on the hunt for new restaurants in my town. I speak on topics that I'm passionate about. I'm always feeling free through a variety of activities that I include in my life.

The next step is to identify approaches to fill your life with these pursuits that empower you to feel those feelings that are vital to you.

Allow the Law of Attraction to take care of the rest. Like attracts like. When you are busy living your life according to how you want to feel, the universe has no other option but to give you more of what you are already feeling.

Do you desire more love? Then, feel and show more love for yourself.

Do you hope for a greater degree of freedom? Your solution is to feel free in this moment to express yourself and pursue what you long for without excuses.

This exercise today is one that (hopefully) will stick with you for the rest of your life. Live your life based on how you want to feel, and I promise you that you'll have a fantastic existence!

Complete the following sentence:
I deserve to have everything my heart desires because

_____.

Day 6

#Dateyourself

"The day you decide to love yourself is the day
you'll conquer the world."
—Unknown

L et's wrap the week up with one of my favorite exercises: the #dateyourself exercise.

Too many people live their lives waiting for some future moment in order to feel a certain way.

Once I pay off all my debt, then I'll start saving for a house.

As soon as I meet the man of my dreams, then I'll take that trip to Bali (with him).

Instead of waiting, NOW is the time to start living the life of your dreams. A primary part of living the life you envision includes romancing yourself, little missy.

We attract into our lives people that treat us just slightly better than we treat ourselves.

Wrap your brain around that for a while.

This brings us to the quintessential question: how wonderful (or not so wonderful) are you treating yourself? Could you use a little BOOST in the self-love department?

Luckily, it's easy to remedy; no matter how well (or not) you are currently behaving towards yourself!

 Exercise: #dateyourself

Number a sheet of paper from 1 to 30. For each number, write down one thing that you love to do. It could be things you do alone like taking a bubble bath or an activity you typically do with others such as going out to dinner or attending a concert.

Once you've put an item for each number on the list, pull out your calendar! Commit to doing one activity a day for the next 30 days. Date yourself. Treat yourself the way you desire to be treated. Then when Mr. Right comes along, he'll simply continue to treat you the way you've been treating yourself.

Stop waiting for your prince to save you! Be your own Prince Charming! :)

Then make it known to the world! Post in the Facebook group how you commit to dating yourself over the coming weeks and months. (Have you checked out the book resources yet? It includes a private Facebook group for you to connect and share with other amazing high-vibe individuals. www.emyraldsinclaire.com/destinationsoulmate.)

Complete the following sentence:
I deserve to have everything my heart desires because

_____.

Day 7

Put Your Feet Up

"Rest is valuable only so
far as it is a contrast."

—Unknown

Take a break! We've put a lot of manifesting power into the universe this week. Truly your only 'homework' today is to continue the new routine we've outlined thus far.

Make sure you are honoring the feelings you want to feel in your life.

Get lost in the visualization and feelings of The One on his way to you now!

Other than that, just have fun! I mean, why else would you be in a body?!

Week 5

LOVE POTIONS AND MAGIC SPELLS

> "Be careful what you wish for
> 'cause you just might get it."
> **—The Pussycat Dolls**

Week five is probably my favorite week in this entire process! This is where the REAL magic happens! You'll learn how to manifest and how to use the Law of Attraction for real. Have you ever wondered how to intend and pray something into reality? You've heard those stories of people 'praying' to win the lottery...and they actually do!

This week is fun, powerful, and really helps you to shift some belief systems and step into the real power of creation!

So, what are the love potions and magic spells, and HOW do they work?

More importantly, WHY hasn't it worked for you in the past? If, in fact, you are a self-help junkie (like myself) and have watched certain movies like *The Secret*, but still are left in the same single situation that you have been in for the past 30 years, what are you doing wrong?

I'm going to help you unravel the big ol' MISTAKE that most are making in their affirmation process. I'm sorry to burst your bubble, but you cannot *only* think positively and expect radical transformation.

And this is coming from a woman who is an eternal optimist and was voted 'Most Likely to Change the Planet' senior year of high school.

Yes, I'm a firm believer in loving the heck out of your life and being optimistic about what is possible because, guess what? Anything is possible.

But…I can't emphasize this point enough…

Positive thinking is NOT enough!!!

As humans (and especially us women), we have a 'secret weapon' when it comes to manifesting that you might have thought in the past was actually something getting in your way.

What's this secret weapon I speak of?

Your feelings.

Yes, the fact that you can be wild, erratic, and an emotional mess at times is a blessing to those of you who want to CONSCIOUSLY CREATE a life of your dreams instead of getting dragged along being reactive to whatever life throws at you.

What you're going to learn to do is HARNESS THE POWER OF YOUR EMOTIONS to help you create the Love Story of your dreams, instead of what has probably been happening to you right now.

Which is most likely a variation of something that has already happened in your past.

Humans are creatures of habit. Whether you'd consciously like to admit it or not, your subconscious beliefs are running the show! For example, if deep down you don't believe that you are worthy or good enough, you are going to attract to you a man who will treat you like dirt so that you can say "see, all men are crap!" Unfortunately it's not enough to *desire* a certain person, because it's the *subconscious mind* (where your belief systems are stored) that is affecting your point of attraction. It's precisely why you can *desire* to be in a relationship but still be single. It's not enough to want a thing. You must *believe* you can have it for it (or *him*) to manifest in your life.

It's a catch-22.

Here's the modus operandi: You believe something. Then you see it. As a result, the belief system is reinforced. And then you continue to attract more of those situations into your life.

Tragically, the vicious cycle repeats itself until you awaken and realize that you must change.

Wayne Dyer once altered a very common saying to read: *I'll see it when I believe it.*

It's the exact same idea in your love life.

Once you start to believe that you are worthy, lovable, and a great catch, then you will attract Prince Charming, who treats you like a Queen.

But until you BELIEVE it, I promise you, you will NEVER see it.

So, are you ready to learn HOW to get deep into your subconscious mind and CHANGE those nasty belief systems that are holding you back from your Happily Ever After!?

Let's go!

Day 1

The Power Of Meditation

"I've always said that prayer is asking, whereas meditation is taking the time to listen."

—Emyrald Sinclaire

Flip back to week 3, day 1, if you would, please. That was the beginning of the process of acknowledging the Evil Stepmother and eradicating her from your mind. For the past two weeks, have you been reading those top 3 power mantras and putting as much feeling as you can into them?

If so, great! Congrats! You are that much closer to changing the programming going on underneath the surface.

If not, it's time to start that process again with renewed vigor. Next, we're going to add an extra magical step to the process. Today, you are going to learn to meditate. Even if you've meditated in the past, I want to stress the importance of meditation in creating the life that you desire.

Our brain lives in four different wavelengths: Delta, Theta, Alpha, and Beta. (There's actually a fifth called Gamma, but for our discussion, we're going to omit that for now.)

Here's a quick rundown. I'm by no means an expert on brainwave activity, but I know enough to get you up to speed. Beta is a high level of brain function and is our normal 'thinking' state. Most of us run our lives in Beta. When you're in a very high Beta, you have issues sleeping and might experience insomnia. It's why so many people with stressful jobs cannot seem to turn their brains off at night. They are in fight or flight most of the time.

On the opposite side of the spectrum, when you are in a deep sleep, you are experiencing Delta. That is when the body restores and rebuilds. In a Delta state, there is no conscious awareness of what is going on. Instead, you are running entirely in an unconscious state.

Whereas a step up, in Theta, imagine a light veil between the conscious and subconscious mind. It's like a small child that you told to pretend to be a dog. Three hours later, he is still barking and running around on all fours. He's highly imaginative and doesn't yet understand the difference (just barely) between what's real and what's imaginary. (i.e., Santa is real.) This is the brain wave state you'll be in when a hypnotherapist hypnotizes you. (And no, it's' not like the shows they put on in Hollywood! Hypnotherapy is actually quite the beneficial healing practice because you can access the subconscious mind and reprogram belief systems...with your permission, of course!)

And finally - Alpha. Alpha is a much more relaxed state than Beta with limited sensory distractions. Close your eyes now, and focus on your breath for about 10 seconds.

Did you do it?

That simple act of closing your eyes removed so much stimulation that you quickly were able to drop into an Alpha state. Of course, you were totally present, but all of a sudden, you didn't have the regular distractions of the outside world vying for your attention.

The point of meditation is to help you move seamlessly and with ease from the highly analytical Beta state into the subconscious mind in Theta state. When you are merely affirming your greatness, you are still in a Beta state of mind, which isn't useful in creating and manifesting the type of change that you truly desire in your heart of hearts. It's the 'whipped cream on garbage' syndrome because you're not actually getting to the garbage, i.e., subconscious beliefs that are going on underneath the surface.

"Whipped Cream"
Pretty sounding affirmations

"Garbage"
Actual Belief Systems running the show

This is precisely why affirmations alone do not work.

It's like Einstein said: *"You cannot solve a problem from the same level of consciousness that created it."*

To effectively use those Powerful Affirmations that we created in week 3, we've got to put ourselves into a Theta state of consciousness.

How do we accomplish this? You pretty much must self-hypnotize yourself. And lucky for you, I was raised by a hypnotherapist.

Today, you are going to spend 5 - 10 minutes hypnotizing yourself so that you can progress into a Theta state of mind. From this level of brain wave activity, then you will repeat your affirmations - your magic spells - to yourself so that they actually begin to permeate your consciousness and start to reprogram your mind, forming new neural pathways. (If you'd like to learn more, I highly suggest reading *Breaking the Habit of Being Yourself* by Dr. Joe Dispenza.)

The Self-Hypnotizing Process

If you prefer to follow along to a guided meditation, go to *www.emyraldsinclaire.com/destinationsoulmate* to follow along using my voice.

I'd suggest meditating in the morning first thing upon waking or at night before going to bed. But definitely avoid meditating in bed as you are more likely to fall asleep!

If you're familiar with meditation or self-hypnosis, you can guide yourself using a process you enjoy or using the one I describe below.

Exercise: Self-Hypnosis

Sit up straight in a chair or on the floor so that your spine is erect. It can be helpful to sit on a pillow or place a pillow behind your back to support you. Make sure you are comfortable and have already gone to the bathroom. Take care of your bodily needs so you can slip easily into meditation.

Rest your arms by your side and close your eyes.

Focus on your breath for 10 to 20 cycles of breathing. By merely closing your eyes and bringing your awareness inward, you've shifted from a Beta to Alpha state of mind.

Now that your awareness is focused within, take the next 10 minutes to imagine the room filling up with water. Expand your senses outside of your body and notice the water slowly enter the room. Continue to breathe nice and slow and simply feel the water as it enters the room and covers the floor.

Keep your awareness outside of your body towards all the corners of the room and feel the water beginning to slowly rise until you can feel it lapping at your toes.

Notice how nice it feels to have the water kiss your toes.

Now, feel the water begin to flow into the room a bit faster so that the water is now at the ankle level. You feel relaxed and enjoy the submersion of your feet in this cooling and restorative water.

From here, the water slowly raises up to your calves and your knees. Now not only can you feel the water caressing your body, but you are also still acutely aware of where the water level is in the room.

You continue to relax even further as the water level rises up to your mid-thighs and your private area.

Now is when you begin to feel even heavier. The water holds you down in your seat, and you feel even more relaxed and comfortable. You couldn't go anywhere if you tried. It just feels so comforting and therapeutic to be in this room with water surrounding you.

The water continues to pour into the room, and the level rises up to your solar plexus and your heart space. You feel calm, relaxed, and entirely comfortable as the water level continues to rise.

As the water inches up your chest towards your neck and your chin, you can't help but notice how good it simply feels to be held and enveloped by the water around you.

The water slips up towards the nose, and you're pleasantly surprised that you can breathe the water in your nostrils without a problem and that you feel even calmer with each and every breath you take.

Finally, the water level reaches above your head, and you're completely submerged in the cooling and restorative waters. The water continues to rush into the room until the entire room is filled to the brim with water.

You extend your senses to observe the water filling the entire room, and you feel terrific, rejuvenated, refreshed, and relaxed in this calming space.

It's as though you could sit here in these refreshing and soft waters for hours or days.

And so you concentrate on your breath, and you breathe as you relax here in this room filled with water.

Continue to extend your senses and notice different aspects of the room around you filled with water.

Continue to breathe.

Now from this super relaxed Delta state, say your affirmations in your mind and imagine the type of person who would believe these affirmations. See yourself as this person as you repeat the statements in your mind.

Allow your mind and your focus to be soft and pliable as the affirmations drift into and out of your mind.

Stay in this state as long as it is comfortable for you.

If time is a constraint, then set a timer for 5 minutes before you are to end so that you can slowly come out of this healing and relaxing space.

Repeat after me: I am a Goddess who deserves to have everything I desire!

Day 2

Practice Makes Perfect

"An ounce of practice is worth
more than tons of preaching."
—**Mahatma Gandhi**

How have you ever learned how to do anything and implement it into your way of being?

Practice, of course!

And consistent practice at that.

Can you imagine doing something once and becoming a pro? While that would undoubtedly be amazing, it's not how our minds or bodies work. We see something. We practice the art of doing something and then eventually it becomes second nature.

For example, do you remember when you were first learning to drive? You read the practicum as to how to drive. You watched the videos. You watched your parents, and eventually, you sat behind the wheel. But did you have to have weeks, months, or even years of practice until it became second nature? Of course not!

Now, if you're like me, you can drive, talk on the phone, and put on mascara all while lost in thought, contemplating a conversation you just had with a friend.

It's become second nature, and we've integrated it into our subconscious mind.

I'd love it if the process of learning to love yourself eventually became second nature to you. At first, it's going to take a bit of practice as you are learning a brand-new way of interacting with your mind and body. But eventually, loving the heck out of yourself and reprogramming your mind to think differently will slowly become less work and more effortless and reflective of your natural state of being.

This week, we continue the process that we started yesterday and work at building a consistent practice that feels good to you that you can do every single day! From here on out, use the practice that we did yesterday as part of your morning (or evening) routine. Add various items from this book that we've already mentioned or will cover in the future and adjust as you desire. You'll know what you need to do to build a diligent practice of tapping in with yourself. You truly do have all the answers inside. You must learn to stop the chatter and listen.

Your practice may evolve over time as you find new bits and pieces that resonate with you. Remember, that's perfectly normal! Some days might be a more extended practice than others, while on other days, you cut it to the bare bones.

As the old Zen saying goes: *You should sit in meditation for twenty minutes every day - unless you're too busy, then you should sit for an hour!*

The most important part of routine daily practice is simply that: consistency.

The second most crucial aspect is connecting with your higher self. Your higher self is pure love. Your higher self knows without a doubt that you are a being of pure loving energy who deserves to have everything her heart desires.

So, how do you connect with your higher self?

You can access her through the practice of meditation.

That's the best way I've found. But other methods involve breathwork, taking mind-altering substances, yoga, and more!

Also, when I'm trying to connect with my higher self, I really enjoy pulling Oracle cards. There is a variety on the internet. If you google "oracle cards," you will find many options, but some of my favorites include the Goddess Deck by Doreen Virtue and the Kuan Yin Oracle by Alana Fairchild. You can't go wrong. Pick one that resonates with you. And use it as part of your daily practice of connecting with your intuition. You ask a question; you pull a card, and you read it and then allow the message to sink in as you need to hear them.

Another process I've found extremely helpful in connecting with my higher self is called "Letters to God." Anytime I've done this process, I've been BLOWN AWAY at the answer it gives.

My client Ciara was working hard to let go of the attachment to her ex. While at the same time still wishing that she could win him back. When she came to me, she knew about the Law of Attraction, but she was still entirely caught up in the 'how.' She was trying to control who was her soulmate and when she would win him back.

She confessed that she was impatient and didn't understand why the Law of Attraction was not working for her. She had a lot of questions that I could not answer for her as I am not a psychic and do not own a crystal ball. But one of her most pressing questions was, 'How do I know if I'm listening to my intuition versus my monkey mind?'

Fabulous question! This question is also one that haunts and plagues many of us.

The following is an exercise that helps you get in touch with your higher self, your intuition, the part of you that knows who you really are.

Exercise: Letters to God

Think of a matter that is bothering you right now. It could be a work situation. It could be the fact that you're single, and you're impatient. Or it could be related to an ex. It doesn't matter what the issue is. Just make sure it's something that's bothering you that you'd like an immediate answer or solution to.

Turn to a fresh sheet of paper in your journal and at the top write Dear God/Universe/Source/Higher-Self/Allah/Big Daddy in the Sky or whoever you like to pray to.

Then go into detail about your problem or issue. Put all your questions and frustrations down on a sheet of paper.

When you're done, write *please answer me through the ink in my pen.*

Sign your name.

Turn to a fresh sheet of paper and close your eyes. Take a couple of deep breaths and completely clear your mind.

Once your mind is empty, start the sheet of paper with Dear Emyrald (obviously use your name) and allow the words to come without thinking.

This is how you tap into the infinite knowledge of your higher self. You're going to be amazed at the answers you get!

Disclaimer: some people take longer than others to be able to let go of their monkey mind and actually tap into their intuition. That's perfectly fine! Just continue to practice this exercise once a day until you feel a shift. You'll know when your higher self is speaking through you.

Repeat after me: I am a Goddess who deserves to have everything I desire!

Day 3

Listen To Your Heart

"Your heart knows things
that your mind can't explain."

–Unknown

Allison had a hard time describing her feelings to me. Whenever I'd ask her how she felt about a particular subject, such as her father or her ex, she'd go into a description of him or past details of their time spent together, but she had a very challenging time answering the question, *how do you feel?*

She was very disconnected from her emotions, her feelings, and her heart.

Now is that so surprising? We've grown up in a time and place where women are considered to be equal to men, and we are forced to be practical, logical and to push our feelings aside. There are so many negative stereotypes about emotional women that even I have had a difficult time connecting with my heart…

Until I simply learned how to listen to what my heart had to say.

One week I gave Allison a simple exercise to perform every day and then report back to me how it went a week later.

I asked her to sit down with her journal and a phone timer. She was to close her eyes and place her hands on her heart and ask, *what are you trying to tell me?*

She was more than surprised to learn that her heart had a lot to say! She told me that it wouldn't shut-up. She sat there for almost an hour with tears running down her face as her heart finally had a chance to tell her how much love there was for her and that she was amazing and smart and why did she keep dating the losers, 'you're so much better than that,' and I love you, I love you, I love you...

On and on, her heart spoke to Allison until she was ready to open her eyes. She sat there, dumbfounded. Crying. And eventually composed herself and started writing. And the words continued to spill out.

She had allowed her heart to speak and, girl, did it have a lot to say.

Listening to your heart is another way to connect in with your intuition.

But not only that, I've found that when I take the time to listen to my heart, the quality of the words are always a bit different than my intuition. It usually revolves around emotions and feelings.

Today you're going to listen to your heart. And if you enjoy the exercise, I suggest you continue to do it as part of your daily practice. Or at least when pressing matters come up.

Your heart knows what is best. Much more so than the ego-controlled logical mind. Stop trying to think everything out. Use your feelings. Listen to your heart.

Think more with your heart and feel more with your mind.

This gets you deeper into your feminine side, which, as a real bonus, makes you more attractive to masculine men. Score!

Exercise: Listen To Your Heart

Set your phone timer for 2 to 5 minutes. Make sure your journal is nearby to take notes when you're done. Close your eyes and place your hands on your heart and ask yourself, *what do you need to tell me?*

From there, all you've got to do is be quiet and listen.

Repeat after me: I am a Goddess who deserves to have everything I desire!

Day 4

Who's Got Your Attention Now?

"Where attention goes, energy flows."
—An age-old adage in the spiritual community

Therefore, what you focus upon surely will multiply and grow in your life.

Have you ever had a string of unfortunate events happen to you? The worse it gets, the worse it gets.

Now on the flip side, have you ever experienced being in the flow and more, and more, and more good would just keep happening for you?

I personally have noticed the magic that happens when I consciously direct my attention to all that is amazing in my life and what I'm grateful for.

Close your eyes right now, and feel the emotion of gratitude. Think of a couple of things or people or experiences in your life that you are grateful for.

There!

Can you feel the energetic shift in your body?

It's literally impossible to be grateful at the same time as experiencing any type of negative emotions. Stress fades away, and all of a sudden, life isn't so challenging.

If it's true that we get more of what we focus our attention upon, then what do you choose to focus your attention upon? Remember you can make a new choice and you can do that right now. Change doesn't have to happen tomorrow. It could occur right now this instant. Poof! Brand new you. :)

When I first started a gratitude journal, it helped to create a certain mindset that spilled over into the rest of my day. I started my day by counting my blessings, and sure enough, more of those same blessings came my way!

Instead of waking up, rolling over, and checking Facebook, why not roll over and grab your journal and start a gratitude list? What are all the things or people in your life that you are grateful for? Instead of worrying about a meeting at work and how it's going to go, why not put energy into the fact that you are grateful for the job that gives you money to put food on the table and a roof over your head?

It's a small shift that can have a profound impact on how you feel and how you run your day.

It's a practice I continue to do to this day, and it's one of my favorites to do!

What I started doing, soon after I began my coaching practice, was a Future Gratitude Journal. I started writing things I was grateful for in the present tense that hadn't happened yet.

Why is this habit so powerful?

The power resides in that it puts you in that feeling state as if the dream had already happened. And not only that, you're putting the confidence out there that you are sure it's going to happen and that you're already grateful that it happened!

148

For example, I wrote desires like, *I'm so grateful for my clients who gladly pay me in full each month. I'm grateful for the five new clients I manifested this month. I'm grateful for the 300 new signups to my mailing list.*

I'm sure you can guess what happened! New clients appeared out of nowhere. They were a friend of a friend and had heard about my work and wanted to work with me! My e-book gained popularity and was forwarded by a couple of key people adding over 300 people to my mailing list that week alone!

Now, those might not seem like tremendous accomplishments, but you've got to start somewhere, and you don't want to write things so outlandish that even you don't believe it can happen.

Also, at the same time, write down those HUGE goals. You've got to start somewhere, and since we are practicing patience, consider this practice as putting your order in with the universe.

I've had wishes come true over a decade later! Who cares when it happens? It's all part of the fun of creation.

A Course in Miracles says: *Those who are certain of the outcome can afford to wait, and wait without anxiety.* So put your dreams down on paper and TRUST in the percolation process!

Exercise: The Gratitude Journal & Future Gratitude Practice

Pull out your journal and write for 5 minutes everything you are grateful for in your life. Small things and big things. Write them all down there.

Once the timer goes off, set it again for 5 minutes and start a fresh sheet of paper to write down all the things in your life that have not happened yet that you are grateful for (in the present tense).

Continue this exercise daily for maximum impact. Put yourself in that grateful state of everything you have and everything that is coming to you, and I promise you, your blessings will multiply!

Repeat after me: I am a Goddess who deserves to have everything I desire!

Day 5

The Power Of Prayer

"The only meaningful prayer
is for forgiveness."
—A Course in Miracles

Some people think that asking for help is a sign of weakness. I think it's a sign of strength. You are drawing on the collective to accomplish that which one could not accomplish alone.

I want to tell you a quick story taken from studies done by Masaru Emoto. Masaru took pictures of frozen water crystals from various sources of water. Generally, clean, healthy water creates beautifully formed geometrical crystals, while polluted water is too sick to form any at all. (See pictures below from: https://www.thcfarmer.com/threads/the-water-crystals-of-dr-masaru-emoto.22867/.)

Yusui Mountain Spring, Japan

Fountain in Lourdes, France

Mt Cook Glacier, New Zealand

Mr. Emoto decided to see how thoughts and words affected the formation of untreated distilled water crystals. Below left is an image of very polluted and toxic water from the Fujiwara Dam. Below, right is the same water after a Buddhist monk (Reverend Kato Hoki, chief priest of Jyuhouin Temple) offered a prayer over it for one hour. Prayer alone restored the water back to its beautiful geometric form.

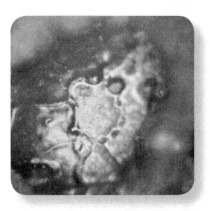

Before, Polluted   After Prayer, Beautiful

I HIGHLY suggest you pick up and read *The Hidden Messages of Water* by Masaru Emoto and prepare to have your mind blown!

Prayer is nothing more than a powerful desire. One could even call it an intention. The trick here, once again, is to remove your attachment to the outcome.

A Course in Miracles says: "Prayer is a way of asking for something. It is the medium of miracles. But the only meaningful prayer is for forgiveness because those who have been forgiven have everything... the prayer for forgiveness is nothing more than a request that you may be able to recognize what you already have."

I have my own religious beliefs, and no doubt, you have yours. The point of this chapter is not to sway you to believe any way over another. Instead, it's meant to remind you that there IS a power greater than you. You ARE a part of the whole organism of the Universe. Think of all the cells that make up your body. Each one has its job to do. Each one is separate and unique, and yet they make up the entirety of the organism of the human body. You are special and unique, and yet you are made of no different materials as Oprah Winfrey or Benjamin Franklin or our sun or far-off galaxies. You truly are made of stardust.

In *Leveraging the Universe*, Mike Dooley makes an excellent point: **you've got to do your job so that the universe can do its part.**

And as someone smart once said, **luck favors those who work hard.**

I like to use the analogy of a cog in a series of cogs. If one cog stops spinning, they all stop spinning. But if your cog takes inspired action and does the little things that you can do, then all the cogs start spinning in unison, and the magic can really happen!

Your role in making magic happen is to do everything that you know to do in your little bubble of reality and then trust that the Universe will do its part.

To paraphrase Thich Nhat Hanh, *Enlightenment is when the wave realizes it is the entire ocean!*

It's time for you to realize that you are the entire ocean, my dear.

And here's how.

Exercise: Prayer

There's a statistic that shows that those who pray tend to have a specific outlook on life. They are more positive and helpful. They don't sweat the small stuff. And ultimately, they believe that everything is working out FOR them, not to them.

Today, you're going to give up so much control and step into the magical flow of your life by using the power of prayer.

I invite you to get down on your knees or simply sit in a chair. Close your eyes and pray. If you're never done it before, there's not much to it. You are merely asking for what you want. You could be asking for healing or forgiveness. It doesn't matter much what you say but that you realize that you are part of something greater than just you, in a body, on this planet.

If you're stuck, try saying the following:

Dear Universe, I ask for your help in healing past mistakes. Please help me to forgive myself and others. I ask for your assistance in living a life filled with joy and love. Please guide me to make the most loving and aligned decisions. And finally, please help me to hear my intuition and connect with my higher self at all times.

And so it is, my dear.

Repeat after me: I am a Goddess who deserves to have everything I desire!

Day 6

I'm Feeling Good

"Birds flying high, you know how I feel. Sun in the sky, you know how I feel. Breeze drifting on by, you know how I feel. It's a new dawn, it's a new day, it's a new life for me. And I'm feeling good!"

—Nina Simone

Dr. Pat Allen once said in one of her books, "a woman must feel good in order to do good." And I must say that I agree! Many women are feminine at their core, and so they are run by their emotions.

However, the challenge of the journey is to learn how to move beyond being controlled by your emotions and instead learn how to use your emotions to control your life! In a fabulous way, of course.

Corey was having a rough go. She had just lost her job. Her washing machine was not working. Her car just broke down. And she was 5 days away from her electricity getting turned off.

"How can I focus on feeling good, Emyrald, when everything around me is crumbling down?!"

I must say she had a good point.

How can you turn your focus on something that is not in your immediate surroundings when your reality is so strong and prevalent?

The answer is practice. Your brain is a muscle, just like any other muscle in your body. It gets stronger the more you practice using it. And practicing where to put your focus takes time and energy.

Instead of looking around at your current reality and thinking to yourself *well this sucks*, you can ask yourself *how can I improve my situation?*

You've now just given your brain the task to look for solutions instead of focusing on what's wrong.

When you focus only on the problems, how can you truly ever find a solution to your woes? However, when you are solution-oriented, you open yourself up to the possibility of a solution.

So no matter how bad you might be feeling right now, I want you to adopt the mindset of *How can things get better? How can I feel better right now?*

And guess what? You actually have an entire list of how you want to feel (week 4, day 5) plus a whole list of activities that put you in a high-vibrational state (week 2, day 2). Right now, at this moment, you have at your disposal the ability to magically raise your vibration based on what you personally know helps you to feel better!

It doesn't get much better than that.

Now, what I cannot do, however, is hold your hand and make you go out and do these things that help you feel better.

That, my dear, is up to you.

Exercise: I'm Feeling Good

Answer the following questions in your journal:

- How can I commit to raising my vibration by doing items on the Love List even when I feel like crap and would rather wallow in my misery and eat ice cream and binge-watch Netflix?

- What could potentially get in my way of feeling better, and what will I do to combat it?

- How could life get better than what it is right now?

- How can I remind myself to look on the bright side and be grateful for everything I already have?

- Are there any people in my life that are contributing to a low level of happiness? Is there any way to change how I interact with them or my feelings about them?

- Are there any people in my life that cause me a high level of stress, and is there any way to remove them from my life, change how I interact with them or change my perception of them?

Repeat after me: I am a Goddess who deserves to have everything I desire!

Day 7

Celebrate!

"Celebrate who you are in your deepest heart. Love yourself and the world will love you."

—Amy Leigh Mercree

Let's take a moment to recognize how many new Magic Spells we learned this week!

You're creating your own personal daily routine with the very real effect of casting magical spells upon your life! Yes, you are the holder of the magic wand, and yes, you do create your future.

You just needed to be reminded of your greatness. And of course, the practical steps along the way to shift from victimhood to heroine!

We live in a magical and beautiful world, and I understand how easy it can be to get trapped in the rat race of what does not really matter: money, material goods, all work, and no play, and a stressful, (but prestigious) job to name a few.

Instead, remember what does matter: friends, family, love, and happiness.

It's so important to use your focus to create magic. You can focus on what you don't want to happen, and as a result, unintentionally pray for what you don't want. Or you can use your powerful energy of attention and pray for what you do want.

Exercise: Celebrate!

Today, we'll wrap up the week with a straightforward question:

How are you going to celebrate your 8-week goal coming true?

Take some time to truly put yourself in the space of your goal coming true. Journal or visualize how you'd like to celebrate.

And then, today, I'd like you to celebrate the progress you've made. Never forget to celebrate the small things, as truly, that is what life is made up of!

Week 6

FROM THE DAMSEL IN DISTRESS TO THE HEROINE IN YOUR LOVE STORY!

> "Whether you think you can or you
> think you can't, you're right."
>
> **—Henry Ford**

It's time for you to learn how to 'step-up' in your life! No more excuses. No more blaming. You are NOT the victim. Pull up those big-girl panties, lady, because it's time to take substantial personal responsibility for your life!

How many times have you ever heard yourself saying some type of variation of the following?

- If only I'd lose 10 pounds, then I'd get more dates and be happy.
- If only my parents had supported me more and paid for my schooling, then I wouldn't be at this dead-end job struggling to make ends meat. No wonder no man likes me. I'm broke and hate my job/life.
- If only Keith didn't leave me and shatter my self-confidence. I don't know if I'll ever love or trust again. It's his fault I'm broken.

This is all bull.

This is 100% giving away your power.

No one has the right to change/control your life except for you and except for those you give away your power to.

NOW is the time to CLAIM your power and recognize that you are 100% responsible for every single situation in your life.

Are you calling out "no way!" right now?

Is your mind racking up various situations where you honestly had no control of the situation and how events played out?

"Emyrald, I didn't TELL my husband to cheat on me! I had no control over that!"

Well, YOU were the one who married him. Why did you marry a man who would cheat? Were there red flags? Did you lose the passion and intimacy and become a nagging mess? Did you two stop communicating, and you became passive and didn't try anymore?

Once you start to take 100% radical responsibility for EVERY SINGLE CIRCUMSTANCE in your life, you'll actually gain a tremendous amount of power.

No longer are you simply the unconscious victim to random occurrences in your life.

NOW you are the powerful heroine in your life, and you'll start to see that EVERYTHING is always working out in your favor, and you ALWAYS have a choice as to HOW to respond to someone's actions. And not only that but last time I checked, you always have had 100% control over the thoughts in your mind and the words that come out of your mouth.

You can simply CHOOSE to see everything as a blessing. Life is working out FOR you, or it's happening TO you. It truly is your choice.

And once you start to CHOOSE to see things differently, the MAGIC begins!

Reading Dr. Joe Dispenza's book *Breaking the Habit of Being Yourself*, I came across a fantastic passage where Joe explains that you can either live in a world of 'cause and effect' of which you simply experience the effects of random causes...

Or...

You can be *'causing your effect.'*

I personally believe we all live in the latter. Whether you believe it or not, you are much more powerful than you know, and you are continually affecting your surroundings based on your perception of what's happening.

Imagine a stranger walking down the street and said to you: "Nice dress."

Do you think to yourself?
A. Thanks! What a nice guy. I LOVE this dress, too.
B. Eww. What a creep. Like he's got a chance!
C. Was he being sarcastic? What a jerk.
D. Oh no! Is there a rip in it? Do I look stupid in this? Did I spill my breakfast all down the front?

Person A is definitely a 'glass half full' kind of person. I would bet $100,000 that she's got a pretty incredible and supportive group of loving friends in her life and a job that brings her joy.

Person B probably got out of a nasty break-up with a man who cheated on her. She also apparently has low self-worth as she's making everything out to be about her. She probably has even gone on plenty of dates with dudes that were so not her type, and then she complains to all her friends that there are 'no good men in this town.'

Person C is distrusting, aggressive, and probably not very happy in life with a minimal support system.

Person D suffers from extremely low levels of self-confidence and is most like a 'giver' who never considers her own needs and wants always going with the flow and doing whatever the group wants to do.

So what is the most significant difference here between the four people?

Their mindset. Their thoughts. Their belief system.

Says one of the sexiest men ever (according to me...and about 1 million girls between the ages of 12 and 18):

"The problem is not the problem. The problem is your attitude about the problem."

- Jack Sparrow (Pirates of the Caribbean)

This week, I'm going to show you how to become the Heroine in your love story, and stop playing the damsel in distress, already! Once that shift happens from rags to riches...your strong and powerful Prince will finally see your light.

But YOU have to be the one to shift into a new woman FIRST before your Prince will come.

Day 1

Letters Of Forgiveness

"Holding a grudge is like drinking poison and waiting for the other person to die."

—Unknown

There once was a woman who perfected the art of holding a grudge, but she was no ordinary lady. Something strange happened every time she got upset at someone and began the process of holding onto negative feelings. An apparent shift moved through her energy field, and the effect was that she became naturally magnetic to the rocks and the earth.

In the beginning, she didn't notice this phenomenon because the transference in her energy field was slight.

However, over time as she grew in bitterness and found increasing reasons to distrust humans and hold grudges against anyone she (perceived) had done her wrong, she observed the powerful effect on her energetic field.

It got to the point where walking became laborious, and eventually, she wasn't able to walk any longer. The magnetic pull to the earth and rocks below her had become too strong after years and decades of holding grudges.

As she stood there unable to move, she only had time to mull over her life and the accumulated injustices and *Look! Now I'm stuck here in this stupid place. Not able to even put one foot in front of the other. Woe is me.*

She stood there for quite some time, stewing over her toxic feelings and emotions. She ruminated for many months and eventually years, focusing on the people and experiences that had mistreated her. She carried the burden of negative thoughts and energy that had inadvertently held her down. These burdens created an incredible additional weight on her energy field so much that eventually, *she turned into stone herself.*

I've said many times in my yoga class: *We don't always choose what we hold onto (energetically), but we can always choose what we let go of.*

Now the question for you, my lovely is: *What heavy load are you energetically holding onto?* Perhaps even unbeknownst to you in your conscious mind...

Do you still blame your parents? Is your boss a jerk for not giving you the promotion? Do you revile or hate your ex? Do you really struggle with loving your siblings? Is it hard to forgive someone from your past who said hurtful things and, as a result, wounded your heart deeply?

Whatever it is, I guarantee you that you have blocked energy in your body because of a lack of forgiveness towards yourself and others.

Learning to forgive (both yourself and others) is an integral step in the process of learning to love and accept yourself for who you are. Plus, it helps to attract an amazing partner to you, which is why you're here, right?

Bitterness is so not sexy.

And forgiveness can be an extremely challenging proposition when you feel life has mistreated you.

If you need to, you're going to start with a simple affirmation, which is: ***I'm open to forgiveness. And I'm open to forgiving*** _____.

Jumping straight into forgiveness can be hard. Especially when we've held grudges for so long and being in an angry state or holding onto the victim role is such a part of our identity. I declare it's time, right now, this instant, to move beyond victimhood. It's your moment to clear and heal your energy field completely. Now you decide that the hurt little girl of yesterday is no longer "you." Instead, forgiveness is the key to embracing and projecting a heart filled with love.

Week 3, day 4, you burned the paper that held onto your yucky stuff that you hadn't forgiven yourself for. Today you are going to forgive others. And if it still feels necessary, forgive yourself some more, too!

If you're like me, you feel resentment towards others in your life. I held a grievance against my dad for not being there as I was growing up (my parents were divorced). I kept a grudge against my stepfather for being a jerk to my mom (in my young perception). I held ill will towards my brothers for being wretched towards me growing up.

Many of these (and other) grudges that I held were unconscious. Somewhere right under the surface. Can you think of any grudges and resentment that you carry?

Until you heal (and forgive) your relationships with prominent men in your life, you will NOT have a healthy relationship with a significant other.

You are doomed to repeat your past for two reasons:

1. **It's comfortable and familiar.** And so you attract what you have grown accustomed to.
2. **Until you learn the lesson, you will keep attracting it into your life.** It's an opportunity to move beyond the lesson, learn, and heal it. Only then will it stop its pattern of repetition in your life.

Today is an exercise that might take a while, but it's essential to do. So please do not skip it.

Exercise: Letters of Forgiveness

Write a letter to anyone in your past that has 'wronged you' that you hold a grudge towards. Some of the most common are parents and stepparents, but it can be anyone really! In this letter, write down all the good and the bad. Write down all the reasons you feel justified in how you feel. Get it all out on paper (and don't worry, no one will ever see it). When you feel like you've had your say, finish the letter with the following:

Thank you for your part in my evolution. Thank you for the lessons. I choose to heal and move beyond these feelings. I forgive you. I love you. I bless you and let this go.

Repeat this process for anyone that you feel like you need to forgive and heal from.

If you so desire, you can also burn these letters and allow the fire to transmute the energy as we did in week 3.

Congrats! You are on your way to a life filled with love, not fear!

I am a powerful creator and I am creating

_____.

Day 2

Your Rosy Love Story

"If we never experience the chill of a dark winter,
it is very unlikely that we will ever cherish
the warmth of a bright summer's day. Nothing
stimulates our appetite for the simple joys of life
more than the starvation caused by sadness or
desperation. In order to complete our amazing life
journey successfully, it is vital that we turn each
and every dark tear into a pearl of wisdom, and
find the blessing in every curse."

—Anthon St. Maarten

Do you recall way back in week 1 when I asked you to write your love story? I hope you did and put a bit of effort into it because today we are going to shift that story so that it EMPOWERS you!

We've all had ups and downs in our lives. But it seems to me that the people who have the most blessed lives are NOT those who have had few misfortunes placed upon them. Instead, it is their attitude and response or reaction to unfortunate circumstances and soul-crushing events that makes all the difference.

You can choose to see everything as a blessing or nothing as a blessing.

Are you a glass half empty or a glass half full type of gal?

Luckily if you're the former, you can easily switch to the latter.

Today it will start with your love story. Yes, it's filled with painful moments and heart-ache. Today you are going to put on your rose-colored glasses and shift your perception of your individual and unique story.

Rewrite your story from the point of view of how EVERYTHING (and yes, I do mean everything) that happened was working in your favor.

For example, my heart was BROKEN when my high school sweetheart and I broke up. But because of that, I grew. I also had no ties to my small town in Illinois and was easily able to move on to a University in Vermont.

Whereas the woman he started dating just after we broke up is now married to him and they still live in that small town. That life was totally not meant for me! In fact, it is totally out of character. What a blessing, you see!

When I had my client Kendra do this exercise, I could literally FEEL her energy change. No longer was she a victim of multiple heartbreaks. Instead, she realized how life was always working in her favor. She was stuck in the victim mentality because she'd been engaged three times, and each time, it didn't work out. She felt duped. She felt like she wasn't worthy and that her Prince would never come. And so she was stuck in a rut of pain and worry.

After completing this exercise, she was able to step into her power. She was able to see what a wonderful life she'd already had and led. Now all she had to do to improve her love life was to shift her perception.

Exercise: Put On Your Rose Colored Glasses

Go back to your love story from week 1. It's time to put on your rose-colored glasses. Rewrite the story only from the perception that everything was happening for you, and for your benefit (and ultimate good). Let me emphasize this!

For example, Kendra was able to reframe the hurt and pain of breaking off her second engagement by shifting to: *Thank goodness I found out he was an alcoholic and broke it off before we got married!*

Once you've rewritten your story only in the positive frame of view, you are only allowed to tell it from this point of view and perspective!

No longer are you allowed to be a victim and wallow in your pain. Instead, you are a powerful heroine who tells her story from a place of empowerment and strength. Life is happening FOR you and never TO you.

I am a powerful creator and I am creating

_____.

Day 3

Mirror Exercise - Part 2

"I am comfortable looking in the mirror, saying,
I love you, I really love you."

—Louise Hay

If I had to guess, I'd say 99% of women do NOT love their body as it is. There's always something to pick apart or wish it were different. I can't even say that I personally love my body 100% of the time! I struggle with breakouts. There are times I feel bloated and fat. I gain weight. I lose weight. Sometimes my clothes fit better than at other times. I'm human, and my body changes.

We were not raised to LOVE our bodies exactly as they are. At least I wasn't. One of my more painful memories, as I was growing up, was being tortured by my brothers. They called me a 'fat and hairy gorilla.' How mean is that?

Consequently, I struggled with a negative body image for years! I was always self-conscious that I was bigger than all the other girls in my class. I naturally had a larger bone structure and a whole lot more muscle, but for a teenager, it was the worst to be about 20 pounds (or more) heavier than all the other girls in your class!

I struggled with bulimia once I hit college. Many women struggle with eating disorders due to low self-esteem. So many of the fad diets around nowadays are actually certain cleverly disguised versions of eating disorders.

This brings me to the question: is it any wonder that many of us carry around extra weight? More than ⅓ of Americans are considered to be obese! Another shocking statistic is that almost 75% of US men are considered to be overweight or obese!

I'd say we definitely have an epidemic of low self-love going on, and it's reflected in overeating or under eating. All with the same goal of using something external to fill up something internal.

I can tell you that I also struggled with my weight on both sides of the equation. When I wasn't bulimic, I was 10 pounds or so overweight. When I was older, my weight would fluctuate hugely! Sometimes as much as 20 pounds in a year. This was when I was not on any diets or being abusive to my body. Something was going on underneath the surface, and I know now that it was related to how I felt about myself.

A surprising side-effect of finding my soulmate (and learning to love myself) is that I dropped 20 pounds in a year without doing anything differently and have also kept the weight off. I finally feel comfortable with my body weight, and I haven't had to do a thing out of the norm - except love myself unconditionally.

It's as though that extra layer of protection that I subconsciously decided to keep on my body had no more reason to be there. I felt safe and secure in who I was and loved by a man who saw the real me. No more protective armor necessary, thank you very much.

How would you like to finally be content and even fulfilled in your body, no matter what your dress size?

I say it's long overdue!

As women, we spend far too much time criticizing ourselves and gossiping about others. Sadly, this unhealthy condition is a result of our own insecurities.

When I was in college, I had an amazingly loving girlfriend named Reina. Reina was (and is) indeed a sweet and kind woman. I cannot think of any other way to describe her. One day we were talking, and she shared with me something that her boyfriend (and now husband) had her do one day in college.

First, here's why. Reina also was extremely self-conscious about her body and suffered from low self-love. She was also 20 years old, so give her a break! Incredibly, her boyfriend offered up an exercise that simply blew my mind at the time.

He asked her to undress in front of the mirror, touch, and appreciate her body as only a lover could do.

In the beginning, she was extremely self-conscious and could not let go of her inhibitions. She simply felt foolish. Ben (now her husband) could see it on her face. He gently asked her to start over. Again and again and again.

Until…

Yes! He could see the difference. Reina had finally (after much trial and error) let go of her inhibitions and saw her body as beautiful, perfect, and lovely. Just as he saw her.

It's time for you to love and appreciate your body for the perfect creation that it is.

Your body is an expression of love.

Gabby Bernstein, in *May Cause Miracles,* talks about her shift in perception of her body. Once she saw it as an expression of love and to be able to use her body to express that love to the world, everything changed!

All of a sudden, she felt a compelling responsibility to take excellent care of her body. After all, the better her body felt, the more she would be able to spread her message to the masses.

You do not need to be a Gabby Bernstein to feel that same responsibility of loving and maintaining your body.

The more love you feel for yourself (and your body), the more love you can share with the world. It's as simple as that.

Exercise: The Mirror Exercise - Part 2

Stand in front of the mirror naked. Yes, naked. Take 10 minutes (minimum!) to adore your body. Notice all the beautiful imperfections. Remember that nothing is really a flaw. Instead, they represent a unique expression of you. Touch your body. Kiss your shoulder or arm lovingly. Trail your fingers down your leg. Gaze into your eyes. Play with your hair. Lovingly caress yourself and say nice things. Imagine that you are gazing at your body through the eyes of your beloved.

It's time to reprogram your mind, love. You are a beautiful Goddess. Own it!

I am a powerful creator and I am creating

_____.

$\mathcal{D}ay\ 4$

Glass Half Full Or
Glass Half Empty?

"Once you replace negative thoughts with positive ones, you'll start having positive results."
—Willie Nelson

How do you change something?

By putting awareness and directing your attention to that you wish to change, considering in what specific ways you'd like to be different, and then taking action to make it happen and finally the process of follow-up and consistently maintaining new habits!

When I was a nutritionist, I'd always have all my clients keep a food journal for precisely one week before our first call together. This was the best way for me to get some insight and clarity into their daily eating habits. What times of day (or night) were they eating? What types of foods? And of course, how did they feel as/before/after they were eating?

Remarkably, I noticed that a pattern had emerged.

Their eating habits shifted mid-way through the week, which was before we even had our first call together.

Why is that, you may wonder.

The primary reason is that they were becoming the observer of themselves. All of a sudden they didn't like how they were eating and they didn't want me to see how horrible their eating habits actually were!

So, when Dawn realized that she was consistently eating sweet rolls or muffins for breakfast four days a week, and was eating chocolate in the afternoons as a pick me up, she changed her eating habits before the week was over. She even told me a bit embarrassed: *I didn't want you to see what I was actually eating!*

This implies that the simple process of observing herself and her eating habits changed how she was eating without me, as her nutritionist, having to say one thing to her about it!

Amazing, huh?

If I asked you if you were, in general, a positive person or a negative person, how would you answer? Most people will say they are generally positive and optimistic.

However, if I was allowed to peek into your brain and look at the thoughts that are tumbling around daily, the truth would be something a whole lot different. We are usually a lot more negative than we think. And at best, our thoughts are 50/50.

So, if you're trying to manifest a wonderful life but your thoughts are contradictory, essentially it's as though you've got two trains pushing against each other with equal force.

A basic knowledge of physics would tell ya that if two objects of equal density are pressing on each other with equal force, that they ain't goin' nowhere.

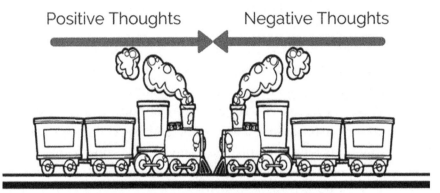

TRACK TO NOWHERE

So, how do we know which train of thought is winning for you? By being the conscious observing of our thoughts!

For the next 24 hours (or longer if you're an overachiever like me), you are going to keep track of your thoughts throughout the day. Self-observation is the only way to know if you're a very positive person or an extremely negative person or somewhere in between.

 Exercise: Notice Your Thoughts

Today you'll bring your journal around with you and do your best to keep a tally of positive versus negative thoughts. Considering we have between 50,000 and 70,000 a day, this is going to be impossible to record and tally them all. I doubt you'll be able to track the 35 to 48 thoughts you are having per minute.

However, you can undoubtedly set your phone timer to go off every hour on the hour and assess where your mind has been over the past hour. Mainly negative? Mainly positive? Middle ground? Lost in work?

The point of the exercise is not to be 100% exact in tallying all our thoughts. But it IS an exercise to help you become more aware of where many of your thoughts fall to unconsciously on a daily basis.

Once we shift from unconscious thinking to become the conscious observer of our thoughts, we put ourselves in a very powerful position to eventually change our thinking patterns to be the conscious creator!

Tonight's Exercise: How Did You Do?

After the day is complete, now what?

Tonight look back on the tally and reflect. Were you more negative than positive? Were there specific triggers that caused you to spiral down into a particular way of thought and being? Are there people that help you feel or think a certain way?

After you've reflected upon your day, you've just taken another critical step. Now you've become the observer or yourself and your thoughts. You've stepped out of being the unconscious body and mind stumbling around in a mess of contradictory ideas and stepped into the power of a person who had stepped outside of herself.

Once you become the observer of your thoughts, you have the conscious ability to change your thoughts. Similar to my nutrition clients, once they observed a specific action, they took the appropriate steps to correct it.

Now that you've taken the time to observe your thoughts, you can course-correct and change the thoughts.

How? We'll learn that tomorrow. So stay tuned...

I am a powerful creator and I am creating

_____.

Day 5

Cancel Clear!

"The positive thinker sees the invisible, feels the intangible, and achieves the impossible."
—Winston Churchill

L et's build on yesterday, shall we?!
A dear friend of mine, Chris Whitcoe, shared an exercise called "cancel clear" with me one day. Chris is an international speaker on conscious business, and he believes it all starts with the power of thought and words. He has a program called "Step Up and Shine," and it's based entirely on the premise of the placebo effect. If a person believes he will get better, then he will. The placebo effect is as simple as that.

So when Chris taught me 'cancel, clear,' I was more than grateful.

He said, "Whenever you catch yourself having a negative thought or saying something that isn't really true (sarcasm, anyone?), you should say 'cancel, clear!' and then follow it up with what you want to say/believe instead."

It's a real-life example of using the eraser on the chalkboard to eradicate an error in your thinking.

Exercise: CANCEL CLEAR!

Today, and from here on out, when you consciously catch yourself in a negative thought pattern such as:

These jeans make me look fat.
He'd never be interested in a loser like me.
I'll never amount to anything.

It's your opportunity to catch yourself and proclaim: CANCEL, CLEAR!

Then repeat 10 times what you do want to believe instead.

These jeans make me look fat becomes: My body is a temple, and I am a Goddess!

He'd never be interested in a loser like me becomes: I'm the prize! The man who is right for me will see my unique beauty!

I'll never amount to anything becomes: I am filled with unique talents, and I can do anything I set my mind to.

Ten times in your head, please.

Over and over and over until one day you've reprogrammed your mind and you're thinking a different way without even realizing it.

I am a powerful creator and I am creating

_____.

Day 6

Lions, And Tigers And Bears, Oh My!

Dorothy: I don't like this forest. It's dark and creepy!
Scarecrow: Of course, I don't know, but I think it'll get darker before
it gets lighter.
Dorothy: Do you suppose we'll meet any wild animals?
Tin Man: *We might.*
Scarecrow: [nervous] Animals... that eat... straw?
Tin Man: *Well, some, but mostly lions and tigers and bears.*
Dorothy: Lions?
Scarecrow: And tigers?
Tin Man: *And bears.*
Dorothy: Lions and tigers and bears, oh my.

How many times have you ever got caught up in your mind? Imagining all the possibilities of what could happen based on your past experiences?

Don't feel bad if you have. We all do. It's part of being human. We have to remember that one time the lion chased us near his den to realize that we shouldn't go snooping around there for food.

Unfortunately, many of us live our lives worrying about future moments, and it's reflected in the present moment of how we speak. And how we speak is the lens through which we observe our life. This repeated pattern - intentionally or unintentionally - affects our future experiences.

Let me illustrate my point with a little story. There were once four men on a safari in Africa. These men were all big wig producers in Hollywood and had plenty of money...and ego to boot.

The sun was going down, and they were there to score 'big game.' The only problem was the tour was coming to an end (because of sundown), and none of them had shot anything yet.

One of them, let's call him Tom, asked, no demanded, of their tour guide to let them stay out longer in the jeep until one of them had the opportunity to shoot a lion or a tiger.

The guide told them it would not be safe with the sun going down and their distance from camp.

But after some heavy persuasion involving a good amount of money, the driver agreed to an hour more.

As the sun went down, the lions came out.

The men were excited as this was their chance!

Fortunately for the lions, none of them were harmed in the process.

Unfortunately for the men, once they ran out of bullets, the Jeep decided to break down. All the bumps through the safari had slowly loosened the battery cable, and they had zero charge and were stranded.

And now they were surrounded by a pride of very angry lions.

The guide walkie-talked an SOS to the camp, and they said they'd send a Jeep asap,...but that it would be about 45 minutes.

Two of the men went into panic mode and started blaming Tom. They were convinced it was his fault they stayed out later. They were all going to die. They hadn't really lived. They had so many regrets. The freak out continued as they got more and more upset at the position that Tom had put them in.

The two men looked to the fourth in their group for support and said: "George, aren't you going to say anything?!"

George replies: "Hmm... This is interesting."

That was it! Interesting.

The story has a happy ending. No lions nor humans were harmed in the safari.

But I'd like to draw attention to George's reaction to the potentially life-threatening situation: *Hmm... This is interesting.*

Would you have had so much composure, or would you have been freaking out as well of all the potential future realities that were certainly awaiting you?

Mark England, a friend I met while living in Ecuador, is the creator of PROCABULARY. The premise is that the words you say and think can massively upgrade (or downgrade) your life. "The words you say [as a reflection of the words you think] can improve your personal and professional relationships, improve your ability to set and achieve financial and time management goals, and be an overall kinder, more productive human being. Your new language will uncover possibilities, opportunities, and help you break through old patterns," as described on his website www.Procabulary.org.

The words you say can either inspire you or literally drain your energy. The same goes for your thoughts.

If you've been dreading a presentation at work all week, how do you feel when you think about it? (Anxious, nervous, upset, on-edge)

If you feel an injustice over how the woman at the store treated you, what are the words you'll say to your roommate when you get home? (Ugh, that lady at the store today! She was so rude to me when I returned the pants I bought last week. She looked at me like I was a crook and was lying. Whatever happened to 'the customer is always right?' Service nowadays. Just isn't what it used to be!)

Our words are a reflection of our thoughts. For the most part, we speak based on what is in our minds.

So if our outside reality can affect our thoughts, feelings, and words, is it then safe to assume that our thoughts and words can and DO impact our reality?

My belief is that YES, our thoughts affect our reality!

Exercise: How Do You Choose To Reframe Your Language?

Today you get to be the most positive person in the world! Today you are going to consciously CHOOSE what you say in every situation instead of running on impulse- and activating old reactionary patterns.

A man cuts you off in traffic? He must be in a big hurry and is late for work! Or maybe his wife just called, and she's going into labor. Wow, how exciting for them!

Stuck in traffic on the way home? Perfect. It gives you time to repeat your affirmations and catch up on that book on CD.

An annoying woman at work is walking down the hall towards you? No biggie. It gives you a chance to practice being open and centered and stressing your boundaries. And maybe she's having a rough week (or year) and could use an open-hearted friend. You never know...

Our words are a reflection of the thoughts in our heads. So today, you are going to change what you say with the end-goal of transforming the thoughts in your head. Which are a little bit more challenging to do. However, you can start with what you say. Eventually, it will work backward, and your thoughts will begin to change as well.

My wish for you is to be able to see the world as always working in your favor, and I promise you it will reflect that sooner than you think.

I am a powerful creator and I am creating

_____.

Day 7

What Have You Created?

"Thoughts become things."

—Mike Dooley

O h, great and powerful one. What are you putting into motion of creating this week? What magic spells and potions have you cast? Are you a whole lot more conscious of how your thoughts and words have an effect on reality?

Today is undoubtedly a day of integration after such a powerful week!

Today I invite you to watch something positive, such as a YouTube video or documentary. You've learned the power of your thoughts, and you know now that you're influenced by everything (yes, everything) in your surrounding field. So be extra careful about the sensory information that you are taking in.

I also invite you to spend some time alone with your thoughts.

Not time in meditation, but merely some alone time with your thoughts. Who is the real you when you're not actually doing anything? Only you can answer this question.

Many people do not spend any time alone with themselves. They are distracted by books or TV or friends.

Today, make time to spend time with you doing nothing. Just sit and be with yourself for 10 minutes. It's not as scary as it seems.

Week 7

MIRROR, MIRROR ON THE WALL... HOW TO BE THE FAIREST OF THEM ALL!

> "Magic mirror, on the wall -
> who is the fairest one of all?"
> **—The Evil Queen in Snow White**

D o you find yourself looking for outside validation constantly? Are you waiting for some future event to validate your worthiness?

Such as:

> *Once a man treats me well and loves the real me, then I'll be happy.*
> *Once I lose ten pounds, then I'll start dating and meet the love of my life.*
> *Once I get a better job and make more money, then I'll feel worthy.*

Far too many people waste their lives waiting for some future events to feel love, happiness, or validation.

So how do you flip it around and LIVE the life of your dreams now?

How do you BECOME HAPPY now so that you meet a man who treats you well and loves the real you?

Why don't you put into practice everything you're learning in this book and start dating now, and then watch the magical transformation as you fall in love, feel secure, and watch those extra ten pounds melt away? (Which is precisely what happened to me when I met my guy. My weight always fluctuated. But once I fell in love, real love, I felt safe and secure. And that extra weight that was a 'safety net' melted away. And even better, it hasn't returned.)

Once you believe that you are worthy and valuable, your fantastic work will be recognized, and you'll be offered a promotion, landing you more money.

Your life is not 'waiting' for you in some far-off land.

YOU are the Queen of your Queendom (today!).

But here's the secret....no searching for your King is required! Instead, learn how to magnetize and shine. Learn the secrets of simply 'being the fairest of them all' (right now), so men can't help but naturally gravitate towards your beauty!

This week you learn how to take action today (and not in some moment in the future that NEVER happens) so that you can BE the fairest of them all.

Get ready for your Prince, Beauty.

Day 1

Present Moment Awareness

"Accept that living in the present moment,
with your present desires, is the best, the
highest thing you can do."
—Deepak Chopra

There are myriad ways on how to SHINE so that you naturally become more attractive to the opposite sex. Or the same sex if that is what does it for ya. :)

And this week will give you six different ways to shift your energetic vibration so that you are calmer, more centered, and ultimately available in your energy field.

Think about all the activities you do daily and the to-do list that always runs through your mind. For many of us, each and every day is FILLED to the brim with activities, and there are plenty of days that we might feel overwhelmed at everything we MUST complete.

Scattered energy creates scattered manifestations.

My fantastic friend, Lakshmi Dev, used to own a yoga studio. It was new, and so she was working hard to promote it and build a consistent client base. At the studio, she always had a variety of events that she was planning each month including my personal favorite, *Women, Wine and Wellness* which involved setting up different food vendors, product samples, and music each and every month. She also had three kids going to three different schools with three very full extra-curricular activities. Oh yes, and on the side, she was an independent distributor for two different companies, and she worked with clients 1:1.

Any time I talked (or texted) with Lakshmi Dev, I would feel exhausted by the end of the conversation just by her telling me about her day or everything she still had left to complete.

A classic example of scattered energy creating scattered manifestations.

I tried to gently explain to Lakshmi Dev why none of her events were truly taking hold. It was that she was trying to put a little bit here and a little bit there, but not truly 100% towards one project. If she put 150% towards growing the yoga studio, or 150% towards developing one (or both) of her MLM companies or hiring a nanny to help ferry the kids around to help her focus upon work, or, or, or! There are so many ways she could have used all her energy towards one or two projects (instead of ten), and I have no doubt they would have been wildly successful.

Instead, after months of trying and trying and pouring her heart and soul (and many tears and bottles of wine with yours truly), she made the tough decision to close the yoga studio. And what's worse is that she still owed almost $40,000 in rent payments that she promised she'd make, but couldn't.

A $40,000 lesson that hopefully, you'll learn from as well as I did.

The question on your lips is probably: *So how do I shift from scattered energy to focused energy?*

Present moment awareness.

How can you shift from focusing on multiple projects such as work, personal life, and kids in addition to thinking about the items on your to-do list that need to happen in the future plus remembering specific ideas, failures, and successes on the path to a single streamlined thought process?

That, my dear, is where your work begins.

It's not as though I snap my fingers and your thinking process is magically changed. It's a constant practice of present moment awareness that is truly going to change your life.

You can practice present moment awareness when you're on the bus or in line at a coffee shop. Instead of looking down on your phone and distracting yourself, I simply invite you to be present and look around you. What is going on in the world?

Too often, we 'hide' behind our smartphone screens.

But I can also share that I've met so many people simply by being present and offering a smile to a stranger.

I was working with Dakota and gave her the task of NOT looking at her phone while she was waiting for an entire week. She was so used to busying herself with Facebook or Instagram. Instead, I challenged her to be open to what life had in store for her if she would just put her phone down.

Halfway into the week, she was waiting in line at a coffee shop, and the cute guy in front of her who had just moved to town asked her a question about local yoga studios. They hit it off. He bought her coffee. They continued chatting. And he asked her out for another cup of coffee over the weekend.

Six months later, they are still together and sharing their hopes and dreams over cups of coffee in the morning.

Do you think he would have felt as comfortable approaching (or interrupting) a woman who was occupied on her phone? I'm going to guess that he would not.

There are plenty of fantastic life experiences passing you by when you're busy on your phone, thinking about the past, or worried about the future.

"Treat every moment as a gift, that is why it's called the present"
—Deepak Chopra

Another positive side effect of living in the present moment is that it's incredibly sexy. When you're not caught up in the 'stories' of your past, and you're not living in a future moment that does not exist yet, you are available to what life has to offer you right now. You are smiling, you are open, you are present. You are taking in the wonder of the world around you as it is right now. Think of a small child who simply enjoys the current moment. It makes you smile just by watching that child enjoy it.

I've worked with plenty of men and asked them what they find sexy in a woman, and their answers ranged from funny, to hot, to laughs a lot, to makes me feel good when I'm around her. They also said they like eye contact, a woman who smiles, and if she seems genuinely interested in them.

If you're not caught up in your thoughts, you are available to make eye contact and really listen to what he has to say. As opposed to being caught up in your head of what you are going to say next to appear smart/sexy/funny/whatever.

If you're on a first date, the task at hand is to find out if the man sitting across from you is your personal Prince Charming material. And the only way you are going to find that out is if you are present to who he is and what he is saying.

Once again, this does not come easily to most of us. We get caught up in either the past or the future.

"Do not dwell in the past, do not dream
of the future, concentrate the mind on
the present moment."

—Buddha

Your task today is to be as present as you possibly can in every single moment. To just listen to what someone is telling you without thinking about your reply. To drive to work and just be present without the need to listen to music or a Podcast.

Can you spend one day developing your "be present" muscle? And then hopefully you'll extend it to the rest of your life.

"Life gives you plenty of time to do whatever you
want to do if you stay in the present moment."

—Deepak Chopra

Exercise: Present Moment Awareness

For only 24 hours (and my hope is you take this exercise longer), you are going to be 100% present to the present moment. Notice times when you are caught in your thoughts instead of being fully here. Remove the everyday distractions and crutches from your life like your smartphone or MP3 player. Instead, just practice the art of being a human being.

Sound good?

Tonight's Exercise: How Did You Do?

Journal how the day went for you. Was it harder or easier than you imagined? What did you learn? What did you enjoy? Were you uncomfortable at times? Did you meet anyone you would not have met if you weren't present? Did you see anything that you would not have seen if you were not present? Reflect on your day for 10 minutes of free writing.

Fill in the blank: _____ is why I am the Queen!

Day 2

The Work

"The Work is merely four questions;
it's not even a thing. It has no motive, no strings.
It's nothing without your answers. These four
questions will join any program you've got
and enhance it. Any religion you have—they'll
enhance it. If you have no religion, they will bring
you joy. And they'll burn up anything that isn't
true for you. They'll burn through to the reality
that has always been waiting."

—Byron Katie, Loving What Is

Today is going to be a challenging day for many, and it will be a day that you are tempted to skip over.

Please do NOT do so.

Today is the day that you will be set free from the thoughts and beliefs that are holding you back!

The premise of 'The Work' is a basis to investigate your thoughts to find the true meaning behind them.

Everything we think and perceive is merely a story. Nothing more and nothing less, but it is NOT reality. It is not an absolute truth. It is a belief system that we attach to a story. And for most of us, we run our lives by stories and are victims of our thoughts and belief systems.

Have you ever thought something like?

Mary should not have told Ashley what I said about her.
Bill should mind his own business.
My boyfriend is a complete jerk.
Lauren should want to hang out with me.
Ron should work on his anger issues.

And on and on and on.

Over 50,000 thoughts tumble through our heads daily, and how many of them are actual truths?

Usually, our thoughts are simply a perception of reality that keeps us trapped in a cage, feeling victimized or saddened or enraged.

What starts as one innocent thought, such as *Lauren should want to hang out with me*, can snowball until you can't stop thinking about it, and your entire day is ruined.

Sound familiar?

> "As long as you think that the cause of your problem is "out there"—as long as you think that anyone or anything is responsible for your suffering—the situation is hopeless. It means that you are forever in the role of victim, that you're suffering in paradise."
>
> **—Byron Katie**

Are you ready to take 100% responsibility for your thoughts and your belief systems and the reality you are creating?

It's a challenging thing to do, and not many are ready for it. But I can promise you, if you make the commitment towards life-long growth, you WILL attract in a partner who ALSO is focused on self-help, personal growth, and living in his or her fullest potential. A soulmate relationship is composed of two wholes coming together, not two halves.

And so the personal growth work is ESSENTIAL if you're looking for soulmate level love. No longer can you play the victim role. No longer can you blame others for what life has in store for you. You MUST take 100% responsibility for your life and every single person, situation, and thought that is in it.

> "A thought is harmless unless we believe it. It's not our thoughts, but our attachment to our thoughts, that causes suffering. Attaching to a thought means believing that it's true, without inquiring. A belief is a thought that we've been attaching to, often for years."
>
> **—Byron Katie**

Imagine if you had ZERO FEELINGS attached to your thoughts. Imagine if you thought the following, and they were simply facts without an emotional attachment. How free would you be?

- Brian got the promotion, and I did not.
- Mary told Louise what I said about her.
- Paul appears to be angry today. I wonder if it's because of something I said.
- My mother is very emotional today.
- My boyfriend decided he no longer wants to be with me.

How radical of an idea to consider not allowing your thoughts to control you because you are attaching feelings to them?

I'm not saying it's 100% possible 100% of the time. But I am throwing the possibility out there that you try.

> ## "If I think that someone else is causing my problem, I'm insane."
> ### —Byron Katie

Exercise: The Work

The premise of 'The Work' is straightforward. It's four questions to ask yourself and answer on paper whenever an external situation is bothering you.

The first step in 'The Work' is to identify the thoughts and judgments that are causing you stress right now and write them down. You can visit thework.com, where you'll find a Judge-Your-Neighbor worksheet to download and print. It is very, very, very important that you write your answers down. (Or you can check out the book resources page, and I've got everything you need right here: www.emyraldsinclaire.com/destinationsoulmate.)

I've listed the questions below to help you out.

Who angers, confuses or disappoints you? Write it in the following format: I am (emotion) with (name) because

_____.

For example: I am angry with Paul because he doesn't listen to me about his health.

In this situation, how do you want them to change? What do you want them to do? I want (name) to _____ _____. For example: I want Paul to see that he is wrong. I want him to stop lying to me. I want him to see that I am right.

In this situation, what advice would you offer to them? (Name) should / shouldn't _____ _____. For example: Paul should take a deep breath. He should calm down. He should see that his behavior is not worth another heart attack.

In order for you to be happy in this situation, what do you need them to say, feel or do? I need (name) to _____ _____. For example: I need Paul to hear me when I talk to him. I need him to take care of himself. I need him to admit that I am right.

What do you think of them in this situation? Make a list. (Name) is _____ _____. For example: Paul is unfair, arrogant, loud, dishonest, way out of line, and unconscious.

What is it in or about this situation that you don't ever want to experience again? I don't ever want _____ _____. For example, I don't ever want Paul to lie to me again. I don't ever want to see him ruining his health again.

Now investigate each of the above statements using the four questions of 'The Work.' This is where it gets fun! And extremely enlightening! You can also go to thework.com to download and print the actual worksheets as I find it much more helpful (and quicker).

As Byron says at the top of the worksheet:

Do you really want to know the truth? Investigate each of your statements from the Judge-Your-Neighbor Worksheet using the four questions and the turnarounds below. Leave out any comment beginning with "but," "because," or "and." Often you will have several negative judgments about one person. Take each judgment separately through the inquiry process. The Work is meditation. It's about awareness; it's not about trying to change your mind. Let the mind ask the questions, then contemplate. Take your time, go inside, and wait for the more profound answers to surface.

The Four Questions

1. Is it true? (Yes or no. If no, move to 3.)

2. Can you absolutely know that it's true? (Yes or no.)

3. How do you react, what happens, when you believe that thought?

4. Who would you be without the thought?

Using the four questions, let's investigate the statement Paul should understand me.

1. Is it true? Is it true that he should understand you? Be still. Wait for the heart's response.

2. Can you absolutely know that it's true? Ultimately, can you really know what he should or shouldn't understand? Can you absolutely know what is in his best interest to understand?

3. How do you react, what happens, when you believe that thought? What happens when you think, "Paul should understand me," and he doesn't? Do you experience anger, stress, or frustration? How do you treat Paul? Do you give him "the look"? Do you try to change him in any way? How do these reactions feel? How do you treat yourself? Does that thought bring stress or peace into your life? Be still as you listen.

4. Who would you be without the thought? Close your eyes. Picture yourself in the presence of Paul in this situation. Now imagine looking at Paul, just for a moment, without the thought, "I want him to understand." What do you see? What would your life look like without that thought?

The Turnarounds

A statement can be turned around to the self, to the other, and to the opposite.

For example, Paul should understand me turns around to:

- I should understand me. (to the self)
- I should understand Paul. (to the other)
- Paul shouldn't understand me. (to the opposite)

Let yourself fully experience the turnarounds. For each one, find at least three specific, genuine examples where the turnaround is accurate for you in this situation. This is not about blaming yourself or feeling guilty. It's about discovering alternatives that can bring you peace.

The Turnaround for Statement 6

The turnaround for statement 6 is a little different:

I don't ever want to experience an argument with Paul again turns around to:

I am willing to experience an argument with Paul again, and I look forward to experiencing an argument with Paul again.

> The turnaround for statement 6 is about welcoming all your thoughts and experiences with open arms, as it shows you where you are still at war with reality. If you feel any resistance to a thought, your Work is not done. When you can honestly look forward to uncomfortable experiences, there is no longer anything to fear in life: you see everything as a gift that can bring you self-realization.

Your turn to do the work!

> "I encourage you to write about someone who you haven't yet totally forgiven, someone you still resent. This is the most powerful place to begin. Even if you've forgiven that person 99%, you aren't free until your forgiveness is complete. The 1% you haven't forgiven them is in the very place where you're stuck in all your other relationships (including your relationship with yourself.)"
>
> **- Byron Katie**

When you do the work, you start by pointing the finger at someone else, because it's always easier to see the faults in others. Quickly you will realize that it's NEVER about the other person; it's always about you. Eventually, you'll come to see that everything outside you is a reflection of your own thinking. This is YOUR story that you're living in, and only YOU have the power to change it.

Fill in the blank: _____ is why I am the Queen!

Day 3

Masculine Vs. Feminine

"Stop it." Isabelle tapped a booted foot in the shallow water at the lake's edge. "Both of you. In fact, all three of you. If we don't stick together in the Seelie Court, we're dead."

"But I haven't."

—Clary started.

"Maybe you haven't, but the way you let those two act..." Isabelle indicated the boys with a disdainful wave of her hand.

"I can't tell them what to do!"

"Why not?" the other girl demanded. "Honestly, Clary, if you don't start utilizing a bit of your natural feminine superiority, I just don't know what I'll do with you."

—Cassandra Clare, City of Ashes

D o you understand that two different energies are living within you at any given moment? And these energies have nothing to do with your sexual organs. Every single one of us has masculine and feminine energy in our bodies. But one of them is usually stronger than the other when it comes to your intimate relationships. And depending on what your dominant energy is, it will affect WHO you attract towards you.

Kirsten is a very strong woman. She's always had to do it on her own. Her daddy never gave her money or assistance (even though he bought her sister a house and gave her brother $50,000 when he needed to be bailed out of a tight spot). Life always seemed to challenge her. And the one time she fell in love... he was taken away from her way too soon. So at some point in her life, Kirsten decided that to 'make it', she had to be a man. She couldn't be soft. She couldn't cry. She couldn't show her soft side. To succeed in life meant to be strong.

So in her 40s, Kirsten consistently attracted very feminine men. You know the type: in touch with their feelings, never wanting to nail down a date, and instead their go-to reply is, "let's just see if it's in the flow."

Kirsten was frustrated with the men in her life and couldn't help but complain to me that 'all men are wimps!'

Which is not the case.

Here is what was going on: Kirsten was so much in her masculine energy that the only men who were attracted to her were the super-soft feminine men.

Opposites attract. Simple as that.

There cannot be two Freds or two Gingers when you're dancing. One leads, and one follows. And energetically, the masculine energy leads, and the feminine energy follows.

It's essential to draw importance to the fact that I'm talking about energy and not sexual organs here. The gay community knows all too well the dynamics of energy regarding attraction. One is the top, and one is the bottom, regardless of looks or what God gave ya.

So in the example of Kirsten, she was so used to wearing the pants, taking control, and handling herself that when it came to dating, she couldn't help but attract in the men who were sensitive and wanted to be taken care of. She just couldn't quite understand how to do things differently, but she was extremely annoyed at the quality of men she attracted to her. And yet, it wasn't their fault. Below the surface, they were energetically attracted to their opposite. And whether Kirsten liked to hear it or not, she was energetically attracting that type of man to her because of the masculine energy she was putting out.

This is where some women seriously start to have issues with the whole masculine/feminine concept.

"But Emyrald, aren't men and women equal? Can't we make the same money and get the same jobs, and aren't we offered the same opportunities?"

Yes! Of course, we are equal as far as pay and opportunity and respect, and love.

But we are not equal concerning energy!

At your core, you have a dominant energy, and that is either masculine or feminine. (With the small exception of about 10% of the population who truly lie in the neutral realm. In which case, if you are not strongly masculine or feminine, you will most likely attract someone to you who is neither strongly masculine nor feminine, either.)

And many women also don't understand if they are masculine or feminine. We start off the conversation, and many women will think they are masculine at first because they enjoy working and thinking for themselves and running life on their own terms. I mean, don't we all?

But when I dig deeper and ask her something like:

Be honest with me, would you rather a man respects your opinion, or would you prefer he listens to your emotions and cherishes your heart and tells you how lovely and beautiful you are? Do you want him to respect your mind or cherish your heart?

When we go a bit deeper, and I ask her to be honest and to place her hand on her heart and listen to what it has to say, guess what response comes up?

The heart!

It's pretty much always the heart. Many women at their core truly only want to be loved, to be heard, and to be seen. They really DON'T need a man that respects their decisions and allows her to take the lead. At the end of the day, a woman wants her man to cherish her for who she is. To create a safe space where she can be herself and be wild and be free to experience the entire realm of feminine emotion.

So in the case of Kirsten, at her core, she was feminine and wanted a man to take control and take charge. She wanted to respect his decisions. She wanted him to be successful and make a bunch of money so that she could just let go and be herself and be supported and told that everything was going to be ok. But she was so used to doing things on her own that she couldn't let go and allow him to lead.

And this is the problem that so many women have today.

Since the women's liberation movement, we've entered the workforce and have become more equal to men in a variety of ways that it's caused a lack of polarity between the sexes. No longer do we have our apparent roles to one another. Instead, I'm just like you. I'm just like him. I can go to the same school and get the same job and even make more money than my man!

Which confuses the hell out of us as a society.

A man goes to open her door, and she says, "I can do it myself, thank you."

A man asks a woman what's wrong and she says, "Nothing, I'm fine. I can handle it." Because she refuses to cry and show her feelings in front of a man.

When there is no clear distinction between the energies, it leads to confusion at best and arguments and a lack of sexual chemistry (and potential break-up and heart-ache) at worst.

So, how do you discern what your real core essence is? Are you masculine, or are you feminine?

Once you figure out who you are at your core, there are steps you can take to ensure that you are entirely in the correct energy when you are dating or with your partner.

Notice that I said dating or with your partner. When you are at work, you are in masculine energy. Simple as that. You have to have direction and set goals. You cannot just go with the flow. You will soon be out of a job.

But in your most intimate relationship, you are going to embody a specific energy and allow your partner to step into theirs.

Make sense?

Exercise: Masculine vs. Feminine Energy Quiz

Read through the following questions and choose the answer that most rings true for you. I highly suggest that you take a few moments to close your eyes and clear your mind. From there, allow the true answer to come up for you as opposed to the answer that you want it to be.

1: When it comes to multi-tasking, I:

A) Can talk on the phone, make a salad and watch the news at the same time

B) Have to do one thing at a time; otherwise one or more of the tasks suffer significantly in effectiveness

C) Tend to be a mixture of both. Sometimes I can focus on multiple projects at once and other times I can only work on ONE project to be successful.

2) When I'm working on a project, I:

A) Tend to get distracted pretty easily

B) Tend to be completely focused and don't notice significant events/noises/other people trying to talk to me

C) I neither get distracted nor become completely focused

3) In the bedroom, I'd more often prefer someone who is:

   A) Physically larger than me

   B) Physically smaller than me

   C) Either; I don't care either way

4) In the bedroom, I'd mostly prefer if:

   A) My intimate partner took control and took the lead

   B) My intimate partner let me take control and surrender to me

   C) Nobody surrenders and nobody takes control

5) Which of the following more accurately describes the kind of intimate partners you've had in your life:

   A) My partners have tended to assume they are right about everything

   B) My partners have told me that they think I always think I'm right about everything

   C) I've rarely had any disagreements with my partners in the past; things tend to go smoothly.

6) At parties or social situations, I tend to:

   A) Get up and dance when the music is on, I like to move my body

   B) Sit and talk with others or watch others tear up the dance floor

   C) Do what everyone else is doing, I don't care either way

7) When my close friend has a problem in their life, I like to:

A) Talk to them about it, listen to them, understand them

B) Solve their problem somehow and look for the solution immediately

C) Think about things rationally and work them through the issue offering the benefits of A, B, and C

8) Which of the following best describes your intimate relationships throughout your life when something is wrong:

A) I close up and shut out my partner, as the tone of their words and intensity of their bodily gestures cause me to shut down, perhaps leading me to stop listening and blocking out their words

B) I withdraw from my partner, wanting to get away from the relationship and even questioning whether I should be in the relationship

C) I'd rather discuss things rationally with my partner rather than wanting to leave or shutting my partner out

9) It would hurt me more if my intimate partner were to say:

A) You are looking tired and run down lately... oh, and have you gained weight?

B) Where is your life headed? You seem to be losing direction. Do you even know what you want?

C) You really treat men differently than you treat women

10) When I'm in a store, and I can't find something I am looking for, I:

A) Ask a store manager or sales representative where the item maybe

B) Look for it until I find it, I don't ask anyone where it could be

C) I don't mind either, whichever is the quickest way

11) It would hurt me more if my partner were to say to me:

A) You've put on weight; you need to eat less and exercise more

B) You're making a bad investment with your money, and I don't think you're really putting in enough effort at your job

C) You're not at all like me

12) After making love, I usually:

A) Want to cuddle with my intimate partner and talk

B) Feel very relaxed and want to fall asleep

C) Go make a cup of tea or read a book or do something else

13) I prefer a partner who:

A) Sweeps me off my feet and is strong, confident and takes charge

B) Is open to me and trusts my guidance

C) Has the same interests and common goals as me

14) I prefer that my intimate partner is:

    A) Stronger and bigger than me physically

    B) Weaker than me physically and smaller than I am

    C) I don't care what they look like or their strength

15) Which of the following situations would frustrate you more:

    A) When I ask my partner what we are doing, they say "I don't know, what do you want to do?"

    B) When I'm driving, and my partner tells me to stop and ask for directions and implies that I am lost and don't know where I'm going

    C) When my partner doesn't pull their weight around the house

Go over your answers and tally up the A's, B's, and C's.

If you answered mostly A's, your sexual essence is more feminine.

If you answered mostly B's, your sexual essence is more masculine.

If you answered mostly C's, your sexual essence is more neutral.

If you have 12 or more A's, then you are highly feminine at your core.

If you have 12 or more B's, then you are highly masculine at your core.

If you have 12 or more C's, you are one of the few in the population who are very much neutral energetically.

Take a moment to re-read the quiz questions.

Notice the extreme differences between the masculine and feminine energies.

Journaling Opportunity:

Imagine taking the quiz from the viewpoint of the opposite energy. Can you imagine situations in your past when you stepped into the 'opposite' energy while in a partnership and the issues it created? How can you commit, over the coming weeks, to recognize YOUR natural essence and to embody it at all times instead of 'switching sides' and thereby confusing the opposite energy that you are trying to attract? Reflect on the masculine and feminine energies and which one you resonate with and how this will affect your point of attraction in the future.

Now What?

Now that you know which energy you are at your core; how does this affect your dating life and relationships moving forward?

This is an essential question because, for many of you, you'll realize what you've done wrong in the past to screw up past relationships.

I personally can share with you the aha moment I had when I first learned about masculine and feminine energy.

I was dating a man who was extremely feminine in his core. At the beginning of the relationship, things were terrific because I had finally found a man who was sensitive and caring.

But after a couple of years with this sensitive creature, I was extremely annoyed and pissed off at him most of the time. He was always late and kept me waiting. He had zero concept of time. I was the one handling the finances and the bills. I was the one running the household. He always wanted to talk about his feelings but never asked me about mine. In essence, he was the girl, and I was the boy.

And I realized years later why I was so upset at him most of the time.

I wanted him to step the fuck up. I wanted to be taken care of. I wanted to be cherished. And at my core, I was feminine, so I was seriously resenting him for being the woman.

Of course, we broke up! He needed a masculine woman who was happy to be the masculine energy! Heck, he even told me once that his ideal would be to be a stay at home dad and have his wife make all the money. Are you kidding me? That should have been the indicator right there that we were all wrong for one another.

But hindsight is 20/20, as they say.

And I learned.

I naturally have a lot of masculine energy. But I'm feminine at my core. So my relationship with my man is consistent work on my end to learn to soften into my feminine core. To ask my man his opinions. To ask him what he thinks and then bite my tongue and wait for him to reply...instead of interrupting with my next fabulous idea.

If you're feminine and looking to attract your masculine counterpart, here are some ideas on how to do so.

- Ask your partner what they think and then listen to their answer. Do not interrupt or respond to them with your great idea. Respect their decisions and thoughts.

- Look good, smell good, taste good, feel good. The masculine energy will be attracted to your feminine beauty.

- Be vulnerable. Learn to express your feelings in a healthy way. Your feelings do not control you. Instead, you can express them as they come up and process them and move through them.

- Allow the masculine energy to approach you. You are NOT allowed to speak first if you see a cutie. Smile; make eye contact, and even wave! But make sure they make the first move and say the first word.

- Practice being receptive. Practice allowing others to take charge and make decisions.

If you are the masculine and looking for your feminine counterpart, here are some ideas for you!

- Ask your partner how she feels. Do not try to fix her or solve her problems. Instead, ask how you can help her to feel better.

- Take charge. Offer your opinions. Speak up.

- Do what you say you will do. Be the person that deserves respect.

- See something you like? Go up to her! YOU have to be the one to make the first move and say the first word. The masculine likes to pursue and go after what it wants. So go get it!

These are just general suggestions. The entire topic of healthy relationships is for another book because I know some of you are still confused because you want to have your feelings cherished AND your thoughts respected. And in a healthy relationship, you will have both!

For now, just trust me based on human attraction and that two opposite energies will be attracted to one another.

Pick your energy and stay in it! At least as far as dating and relationships go.

Fill in the blank: _____ is why I am the Queen!

Day 4

Choose Love

"Because I always have a choice,
I choose love"

—Deepak Chopra

I'm a big Deepak Chopra fan. He throws down some amazing nuggets of truth, and I think what he said up there sums it up perfectly.

Choose love. Simple as that.

I know, I know. It's not as simple as that. Especially after a lifetime of experiencing life. People lie. Our parents unknowingly mislead us while they are looking out for us. We unfairly get fired or looked over for a promotion. A partner cheats. Another stays when she doesn't really want to. The list goes on and on.

So how the heck do you simply *choose love* no matter what?

Well, I considered starting this chapter with a different quote that is way overused but oh so pertinent to the topic:

> The day came when the risk to remain tight
> in a bud was more painful than the risk it
> took to blossom.

—Anais Nin

It's a quote that I think you should post somewhere in your house where you'll see it every single day. Especially if you're one of those who are having a problem staying open to the possibility of love.

You can choose to put a wall around your heart (like I did for so many years). But guess what? You will not experience a deep, profound, and trusting partnership.

You can choose to resist being vulnerable and close your heart and, sure, you'll never get your heartbroken, but you also won't know what it's like to dive deep with a partner and experience what it feels like to know that someone else sees the *real you* and loves you *because of* your flaws.

Every day is a choice, and you can choose to block your heart to love.

Or (and this is my personal preference), you can *choose love.*

You get to make the important and brave decision to open your heart to love *even though* it's been bruised, broken and ripped out of your chest and smashed into a million pieces on the floor like broken glass.

You get to declare to the universe that no matter how many times you've fallen, you still choose to get back up again.

Why?

Because you may not be perfect and you may make mistakes, but the only way you are going to experience the type of love your heart craves is to commit to being open and vulnerable *no matter what* over and over again.

I'm reminded of a scene in the movie *He's Just Not That Into You.*

Gigi and Alex are hanging out at his apartment. Gigi gets the wrong idea that Alex is into her. So she basically jumps him and starts kissing him. He pushes her away and pretty much says, *"Woah, what's going on here?"*

Gigi, of course, is embarrassed because she thought he was into her. And Alex gets upset and exclaims: *"What have I been saying since I met you? If a guy wants to date you, he'll ask you out. Did I ask you out?"*

"No," says Gigi.

"Why would you do this? Why do girls do this? Why do they take every little thing a guy does, build it up in their minds and then twist it into something else? It's insane!"

To which Gigi replies (and I think this is brilliant, by the way):

"I'd rather be like that than be like you. I may dissect each little thing and put myself out there too much, but at least it means I still care. You think you've won because women are expendable to you. You may not get hurt or make an ass of yourself that way. But you don't fall in love that way either. You have not won. You are alone, Alex! I may do a lot of stupid shit, but I know I'm a lot closer to finding someone than you are."

BAM.

So, my love, today I encourage you to embrace your inner Gigi and make a vow to yourself to remain open no matter what. To decide that the quest for open-hearted love is much more relevant to you than winning a game that is not meant to be played. Or won, for that matter.

You don't *win* when it comes to love or other peoples' hearts.

Instead, it's a continual process of opening up and of letting go.

Exercise: Keep Your Heart Open

Today you are going to write a promise to yourself in your journal. Today you'll make the commitment to yourself to open your heart to love and possibilities no matter how much it has been hurt in the past. Today you commit to loving yourself and loving others. No matter what.

For example:

I, Emyrald Sinclaire, promise to open my heart up to love and all the wonderful and exciting ways that love can present itself to me in my life. I commit to taking daily action steps toward loving myself and forgiving others. I know that when I let go of past hurt and pain, I give myself more space to receive additional love. Today and every day, I remind myself that the most essential thing in my life is love: love of myself, and love of others.

Help me to remember to listen to my heart daily and follow her desires.

Help me to open up and expand my capacity to love beyond what I think is even possible!

And allow me to see the love in each and every person and within every situation.

With Love,
Emyrald

Fill in the blank: _____ is why I am the Queen!

Day 5

A Meditation A Day Keeps The Doctor Away

Meditation is the discovery that the
point of life is always arrived at in
the immediate moment.

– Alan Watts

Have you heard of this new-age thing called meditation? Ok, I'm only slightly being a smart-ass. You'd have to be living under a rock to have not heard of meditation. And I've already talked about it at least once in the book so far. And I'm 99.99% positive that meditation has been around since the beginning of man on this planet. Although some of the earliest written records of meditation (Dhyana) come from the Hindu traditions of Vedantism around 1500 BCE.

The benefits of meditation are vast and include stress reduction, alleviation of anxiety, better knowledge of self, improved concentration, and a sense of purpose and connection to something beyond yourself.

And the benefit of meditation that is most effective for you, dear reader, on your quest towards Happily Ever After is the last one: a sense of purpose and connection to something beyond yourself.

Suffering is due to our disconnection with the inner soul. Meditation is establishing that connection

—Amit Ray

I'm sure you're kinda wondering what the heck mediation really could do with manifesting your soulmate.

Well, true love and happiness is an inside job.

We get what we give, and the world is only a reflection of what is going on inside of you. So if you're calm, cool, and collected (in addition to having an active spiritual practice and an understanding of your purpose on the planet plus the connection to the big Kahuna in the Sky) you're going to be a very different grasshopper than the one you were before meditation.

And this new shiny grasshopper is going to jump with a completely different crowd.

High-quality people are few and far between, unfortunately. This is why I know part of my huge mission is to inspire people to wake the eff up! It's time for the Divine Feminine to rise up on this planet and help strike balance. As Tom Hanks said in Apollo 13, *Houston, we have a problem.*

So back to meditation.

Every single morning, rain, or shine, I start my day with meditation. And I can tell ya, on those days where life got too busy, or I had an early appointment and skipped my mediation (I'm human also, ya know!), everything kinda goes to hell in a handbasket. I tend to freak out more, I'm not as chill, I take things out of context, and I'm more likely to be a bitch to my man.

Crazy, huh?

But when I start my day with a very conscious practice of meditation plus journaling plus listening to inspiring messages from people like Abraham Hicks or Tony Robbins, it's as though I'm putting a protective shield around my body and no bullshit can enter!

Today, my morning practice is around 60 minutes. I consider it my investment in myself and my happiness and my continual personal growth towards the most amazing, loving, and extraordinary life ever!

But you can start with 5 or 10 minutes.

The morning routine I've created has been cultivated over the years. Some mornings I do a condensed version, and other mornings, I could sit and pull Oracle cards and journal and meditate until the middle of the afternoon. Been there, done that.

I know this chapter is all about cultivating a meditation practice and the massive benefits that happen to you as a result, but I also want to give you a little insight into all the various aspects of my entire morning practice. It's designed to 'get my mind in the game,' so to speak. And it's the exact same goal for you!

It's time to release the baggage and the drama. Stop worrying about the little things. (It's all little things, by the way.) And step into your true power as a spiritual being having a human experience.

We are but a little speck of consciousness in a body that is part of the greater consciousness of the whole. I love that little analogy that talks about a drop of water in the ocean. That is what you are, dear child. You are a drop of water in the infinite ocean of consciousness.

It's time to reconnect and remember that you are the ocean.

Today you are going to create a daily morning practice that works for you, and you are absolutely required to make meditation a part of it. I don't care if you sit still and try to quiet your mind for only 2 minutes. That is progress. And one day you will be able to sit still for an hour. Trust me.

My current practice looks something like this:

- **Pull Oracle Cards** - There are various decks that I LOVE, and I'll go through phases. The point of the Oracle cards is to help you connect with your intuition. So I'll ask a question such as, *what is it that I need to hear today* and then I'll close my eyes and pull a card. I'll allow the message from the card to be my starting point as to what I needed to hear. And I tell ya, it's incredible! The messages are always spot on, and I hear what I need to hear.

- **Gratitude** - I start journaling about all the things I'm grateful for in my life. Past, present, and future. This practice usually extends throughout my day in my mind. As I'm driving my car. In yoga class. While hangin with my man. You get the idea.

- **Listening to a Guided Meditation** - Right now, I'm digging on Abraham Hicks and any of the meditations to get into the vortex. 15 minutes of pure bliss.

- **Desired Outcome** - There are always 2 or 3 big goals in my life that I'm focusing upon. I have them written down in my journal. What I do is set my phone timer for 2 minutes and put myself in a state of excitement as if that goal has already happened! I'll pretend and pretend and pretend it's just arrived and holy, crap, Batman, I feel fantastic! I'll do this for one, two, or three goals.

- **Meditate Again** - Now, I set my phone timer for anywhere between 5 and 30 minutes and just listen. I've done a bunch of work before getting the juices flowing and connecting to source, so now it's my time to listen to what source has to say.

"Prayer is asking for help, meditation is listening to the answer.

There are plenty of other things I've incorporated into my morning mindset practice in the past, and no doubt it will change in the future. Things like free-writing, journaling, dancing, yoga, visualizing and more.

You've got to find what works for you, but if I could stress one thing and one thing only - it would be MEDITATION.

Understood?

Once again, the point here is that you are taking time to clear your mind and focus on what you want to happen in your life. You are consciously taking charge of connecting to your higher self.

And the benefits of this little morning practice are huge! It will transform your life. Take my word on it, sister.

 Exercise: Craft Your Daily Practice

Take some time to craft a daily practice. Maybe it's as simple as looking up a guided meditation on YouTube. Or perhaps you set your phone timer for 5 minutes and close your eyes and focus on your breath and work on getting the hang of the meditation thing on your own. Perhaps you already own Tarot cards and would love to connect with them again. Maybe you want to write down some affirmations and repeat them in your head. The time is NOW to deepen your connection to something greater than you.

As a result, you will be happier, spiritually healthier, and so much more ready to be with a life-long partner. (For additional support in crafting your daily mindset practice, be sure to visit the book resources at www.emyraldsinclaire. com/destinationsoulmate.)

Fill in the blank: _____ is why I am the Queen!

Day 6

Loving What Is

"I am a lover of what is, not because
I'm a spiritual person, but because it
hurts when I argue with reality."

—Byron Katie

B yron Katie is one of my all-time favorite mentors, and I highly
suggest you read her book *Loving What Is* if you haven't already.
I'm probably going to quote half her book in this chapter, so
you're almost there!

Byron Katie's most significant premise in her book, *Loving What
Is*, indicates that all pain stems from the wish that things were different
than they are at this moment.

"The only time we suffer is when we believe a
thought that argues with what is. When the mind
is perfectly clear, what is ...is what we really want."

—Byron Katie

And my personal favorite:

> ## "There's only one thing harder than accepting this, and that is not accepting it."
> ### —Byron Katie

What a radical thought, huh?

Can you imagine how much brain space (and emotional space) you have wasted in your life wishing things were different than they actually were? How much time you've spent living in the past and worrying about the future instead of merely being present with the here and now?

> ## "Do not argue with reality. I realized that it's insane to oppose it. When I argue with reality, I lose—but only 100% of the time."
> ### —Byron Katie

Guess what?

Whatever is happening is happening. Simple as that. You cannot change reality as it is. So far, in this book, I've taught you some pretty powerful tools to improve your potential future reality. But look around you. This is what you've got, kid. And the sooner you learn to accept it, the oh-so-much happier you will be, darling.

Now that we've cleared that up…

1. **How do you go about not only accepting the present moment but actually being present? And how the heck does that relate to manifestation of true love?**

Valid questions.

Let's address them, shall we?

How do you go about accepting the present moment and living in the present moment?

To accept the present moment does not take much work. For me, it's a mantra that I repeat in my mind when I realize I'm resisting what is.

It is what it is. This, too, shall pass.

It brings me right back down to the present moment, and the chatter stops in my mind for a while. It takes the consistent practice of reminding myself that it is what it is. I can't change it. So why worry about it or complain about it?

2. How do you live in the present moment?

It's simple, really. You shut your brain up. Know the best way to do that?

Meditation.

Boom. Told ya, this would come up again.

You learn to control the runaway horse carriage that we'll call your mind and stop getting caught up in your thoughts.

Instead, you slow down. You stop multitasking. You put away your phone. And you just are. You're a human *being*, remember. Not a human *doing*.

And for some of you, this is going to be freakin' huge! And by huge, I mean difficult to do. How does one live in the present moment when we've all been raised with the bright, flashy object syndrome? Our attention is continuously battled for. And to be the person present to the current moment is undoubtedly to be the odd man out.

"The man who follows the crowd will usually get no further than the crowd. The man who walks alone is likely to find himself in places no one has ever been."

—Alan Ashley-Pitt

Present moment awareness starts right here and right now.

Put the book down and look around you. What's going on? What do you see? How quickly do the thoughts come back into your mind? Now slow things down and spend a full minute just noticing one thing in the room. Pick an object and take it all in. The colors of it. The shape. The texture. The smell.

Go ahead - do it now for a full minute.

Congrats! You did it. That is present moment awareness. And the more you can string those moments together, one after the other, the better person you will be and the more highly you will be sought after.
How can I say that?
That relates to the question from above:

How the heck does present moment awareness and accepting what is related to the manifestation of true love?

Well, let me ask you this:
Would you rather the person sitting across the dinner table from you were actually listening to everything you had to say and was making eye contact and fully engaged in the conversation and what you had to say or not really paying attention and instead thinking about their reply (or something else they had to accomplish that day)?
I'm pretty sure we would all prefer that our friends/lovers/dates/ etc. were actually fully present to us and what we were saying. And presence is sexy.
Let me share with you another little fun fact:

Many people will like you because you're a good listener and let them talk.

Yup. Studies have proven that the more questions you ask about someone else to get to know them AND listen to their replies, the more likely they are to rate you higher on the likeability scale. (Don't believe me? Read *How to Win Friends and Influence People*. An oldie but a goodie.)

Ya gotta cultivate that present moment awareness to help increase your likeability.

And I don't think it's shallow at all. Because it's also a spiritual practice that is going to serve little ole you in the long run.

 Exercise: Present Moment Awareness

Today you're going to do your damnedest to be present as much as you can. Notice how often your mind wanders with worry or anxiety. Notice how often you interrupt someone (and why, for that matter). Can you put the iPhone down and just enjoy the walk or your lunch or the bus ride, already?

Good luck. Let me know how that goes for ya.

Tonight's Exercise: How Did You Do?

How did you do? Did you find it incredibly challenging (and annoying AF) to practice being present? Or did you love the challenge? If it's your first go at it, you probably forgot all about the exercise that I assigned to you. Never fear, you can try again tomorrow. And the day after that. And the day after that. And the day after that.

Tonight, here are two exercises for you:

Part 1: Reflection

Pull out your journal and free-write. How did today go for you? What did you notice about yourself? Are there habits you would like to change? Are you embarrassed about certain unconscious (but now conscious) habits that you'd like to change?

It's all good. Everything you write is perfect. Don't judge yourself. Just be aware of yourself.

Part 2: Meditation

Ooooh, you knew this was going to come up, didn't you?

You can follow along to my beautiful voice using the guided meditation I've provided you on the website, or you can read below, memorize it and do your best to remember.

Guided Meditation

Get comfortable in your meditation space and close your eyes.

Focus on your breath and take slow inhalations and exhalations out of the mouth.

Let go of those thoughts of the day and bring your undivided attention to your breath.

There's nothing more important at this moment than your breathing. Become aware of it, and enjoy it and appreciate it.

Sit here for the next minute or so, focusing upon your breath. You have nothing more to do than simply be present. Noticing what is happening in the body as you breathe.

Inhale.
Exhale.
Inhale.
Exhale.

(sit still for a while longer in this space)

Now, as you inhale say, silently in your own mind, *I breathe in love.*

And as you exhale, say, silently in your own mind, *I let go of fear, doubt, and worry.*

Inhale love.

Exhale fear, doubt, and worry.

Continue this cycle of breathing and repeating in your mind for as long as it feels right for you.

When you're ready, open your eyes.

And have a fabulous night, my love.

Fill in the blank: _____ is why I am the Queen!

Day 7

Free Day!

"In all of living, have much fun and laughter.
Life is to be enjoyed, not just endured."
—Gordon B. Hinckley

Yeah! Free day! You covered a lot of ground this week, so today is your day to take a break and do what you want to do! Do you need to catch up? Do you need to review your notes? Do you want to spend more time in meditation and reflection? How about a nice walk in nature? Would you like to practice being more present?

Only YOU know what you need. Make sure to give yourself that today.

You deserve it, Goddess!

Week 8

THE CARRIAGE RIDE TO THE BALL

"Would you tell me please, which way I ought to go from here?"
    says Alice.
"That depends a great deal on where you want to get to," replies the
    Cheshire Cat.
"I don't care much where," says Alice.
"Then it doesn't matter which way you go," states the Cat.

—Lewis Carroll, Alice in Wonderland

This passage above illustrates a beautiful point. If you don't care where you're going, then it doesn't matter which way you go.

But by now, things should be a whole lot different for you, my friend! You have a pretty darn good idea of where you're going and where you'd like to be, and I've given you the tools to get there!

Over the past seven weeks, you've learned a lot of new skill sets. You've learned to take control of the thoughts running rampant in your mind. And NOW you're the heroine of your life's journey. It's time for the climax of your own personal love story.

You've worked hard to become the Princess that you know you are.

Learn the final transformation… get into the carriage… and get on your way to the ball!

In this final week, you'll learn the skills to pull everything you've learned together and to create a roadmap towards the destination that you most desire.

After all, your Happily Ever After is waiting!

Day 1

Behold! The Almighty
Vision Board

"When I was young, it seemed that life was so wonderful
A miracle, oh it was beautiful, magical
And all the birds in the trees, well they'd be singing so happily
Oh joyfully, playfully watching me
But then they sent me away to teach me how to be sensible
Logical, oh responsible, practical
And they showed me a world where I could be so dependable
Oh clinical, oh intellectual, cynical."

—The Logical Song by Supertramp

When we are young, the entire world is a dream. We play pretend. We dress up and imagine we are superheroes in far off lands. And then somewhere along the way, we are told to be realistic. To put our heads on straight. To grow up. To get a job. And to get our heads out of the clouds and back to reality.

Have you ever heard anything along those lines from your parents?

Luckily my parents were very supportive of me doing whatever it is that I desired to do. In fact, my Dad read *Oh the Places You'll Go!* to me every night as a child. The imprinting was deep. Instead of being taught to be 'logical,' I was inspired to dream up whoever it was that I wanted to be.

And as my Mom remembers, I wanted to be a 'mailman on the moon.'

Some dreams never die. I still want to travel to outer space.

Do you still have dreams? Do you dare to allow your heart to whisper them to you? Or have you long been crushed by reality and society and your parents, and now you're realistic about what you desire to have in your life?

Don't try to be too much or have too much or do too much because most likely, it won't happen, and you'll be disappointed, and your ego will be crushed, and you'll feel like a big fat loser.

But you want to know what I think a loser is?

I think a loser is someone who has dreams and goals and desires and NEVER goes after them.

A winner is someone who falls down nine times and gets up ten.

Maybe I just have an abnormally large faith muscle, but I believe in the power of my dreams, and I will never give up until I have the life of my dreams. I KNOW my desires were given to me for a reason. They are mine. And they are pointing me to the best version of myself that I can possibly create.

The big guy in the sky did not create you so that he could dangle a carrot in front of you that is out of your reach.

What you desire shall be yours.

Simple as that.

If you want it, it's because you have the ability to have it.

If your imagination can create something first in your mind, then you can manifest it into your reality.

Our subconscious minds are highly visual. When we are *looking* at something, a specific part of our brains lights up. When we close our eyes and *remember* what we just looked at, the same part of our brains light up. And when we close our eyes and play *pretend and imagine* something, the same part of our brains light up!

Our brains don't know the difference between reality, memory, and imagination. Because honestly, there is no difference. Everything starts in our brain first. You have to have the ability to see it first in your mind's eye before you go about taking the practical steps to create it. *Am I right?*

You know that you have a subconscious mind, yes?

Good. Most people do. However, many do not understand its power beyond that.

The subconscious mind is like a hidden second mind. And this second mind is where all of our belief systems are stored. And for many of us, we are not aware that we have actually created our belief systems due to thoughts we've habitually thought throughout our entire lives.

Our subconscious mind is very much like a fertile garden. And the seeds that you plant in the garden are your habitual thoughts, which turn into your belief systems. The subconscious mind carries out our subconscious programming into our conscious reality. These programs can be either positive or negative. Whenever you observe a limiting belief play out in your life, you have the opportunity to change it. For example, the thought, "I am not good enough," or "I don't believe in myself," are such limiting beliefs that come from negative subconscious programming. Have you ever caught yourself thinking anything negative? I'm sure you have! And today, you're going to learn how to change that programming by giving your subconscious brain something else to focus upon.

Sticking with this analogy, the conscious mind is the gardener tilling the soil and maintaining the plants.

So, if the subconscious mind is hidden, how do you control what thoughts get planted and fertilized?

Excellent question, my dear.

The conscious mind has the power because your conscious mind is the gardener. The conscious mind can rip out weeds and care for the plants that he/she wants to grow instead. But many of us never knew the role of the conscious mind. It's a very powerful one, indeed. The subconscious mind, on the other hand, does not discriminate. Whatever thoughts come its way, it shall plant. If you repetitively think a certain way, whether these thoughts are positive or negative, it will allow them to grow. But the conscious mind, aka the gardener, is the one who has all the power to choose which plants shall flourish and which shall die. This is why it's so important to be conscious of your thinking.

Once you truly embrace this idea, you will be very careful about the thoughts you think and the *images* you allow to pass into your brain.

And that is what today is all about: the power of visualization and how it relates to the subconscious mind.

What is visualization? It's holding an image in your mind over and over for a certain amount of time.

Aristotle, back in ancient Greece, supposedly said, *"The soul never thinks without a picture."*

Similar to an affirmation where you repeat a phrase over and over, time after time, the visualization is a message you are giving directly to your subconscious mind, whose language is that of images and emotions.

The key to visualization is to put yourself in the feeling state of what you desire, having as if it has already happened. Ready for the love of your life? Imagine in your mind the two of you in a loving embrace. Feel his arms around you and feel the love, baby.

Instead of massaging your *hope* muscle, which sends out a message of *lack*, you are massaging the muscle of visualization and *faith* that it is already happening for you at this very moment.

Remember: the subconscious mind cannot differentiate between what it sees and what is imaged. Your subconscious mind is going to get to work on creating the reality that you are putting in front of it.

Exercise: Create a Vision Board

This is an amazingly powerful exercise because you are speaking directly to your subconscious mind via images and emotions.

Today you're going to create a vision board. You can do so with magazine clippings on a large board. Or you can use technology and a platform like Pinterest to pin yourself the life of your dreams.

A vision board is a visual representation of a desired feeling or situation made up of images, symbols, affirmations, and words.

First things first – set an intention for your vision board. The first time I made one, I fasted for three days. I got all my materials together and went to work manifesting the love of my life! I listened to Dr. Pat Allen (relationship guru) while I was working and allowed all my dreams and emotions and feelings to pour into the board. I was consciously creating the love of my life, for crying out loud!

Next, get yourself comfortable. Many people will go the old-fashioned route and use magazine clippings or print out images from the computer. Others will write/draw directly on their board. There is no wrong way to make a vision board. Instead, all you have to do is make sure the board conveys a strong emotional feeling to it of what you are looking to create in your life.

A Vision Board serves as a road map to your deepest desires. It reprograms your subconscious mind.

Once you are done with your board (and it doesn't have to take you three days as it did for me), place it somewhere where you'll see it every day. Set aside five minutes a day to stare at the board and allow yourself to FEEL all the emotions that this board brings up for you.

You are reprogramming your subconscious mind to get to work to create the reality you desire consciously.

Well done, you!

Repeat after me: I love myself, and I deserve to have everything my heart desires!

Day 2

Fake It 'Til You Make It

"What you put out is already on
its way back to you."

—Oprah

You get what you give. You get what you expect to receive. You get to have it all...

If you believe that 'it all' is on its way to you.

Have you ever heard of the expression "fake it 'til you make it?"

I sure hope so because that is what today is all about.

Remember yesterday when we discussed that the subconscious mind is both visually aligned and emotionally aligned?

You can *consciously* plant seeds in your subconscious mind by using images or feelings.

And today, we are going to use the power of storytelling to invoke emotion within your body and subconscious mind to create the love of your life.

Have you ever read a book or watched a movie, and it invoked a specific emotion with you like rage, anger, happiness or sadness? Haven't you ever left a comedy with a lighter step and a smile on your face? Or read a trashy romance novel and had your heart pick up its pace when you're in a racy passage?

The body physically responds to thoughts and emotions. And so does your subconscious mind.

Today, we'll use a process called Workshopping that I learned from the amazing Abraham, channeled by Esther Hicks.

Workshopping is a fancy term for 'fake it 'til you make it.'

Exercise: Workshopping

Grab your smartphone. (What? You don't have a smartphone? Grab a tape recorder or some type of device where you can record yourself speaking.) You are going to create a scenario and tell the story that it just happened. If you're trying to manifest the love of your life, I want you to tell the story of meeting him/her with so much emotion that when you play the recording back to yourself, even *you* believe it. You hear me? Put emotion into it. You are going for the academy awards, here. And the prize? True love.

Then your mission is to listen to this recording every day until it manifests. Or until you get bored. Then you'll simply create a new story that invokes a whole lotta emotion within you. You are giving your subconscious mind new thoughts to plant. And then your conscious mind is going to reap what you sow, baby!

For example:

Oh. My. Gawd. Lorie. You will not believe what just happened! I just met an amazing man, and he's everything I've been asking for! He's sweet, sexy, funny, and has his own place in Telluride! We just spent all weekend skiing and cooking together. He LOVES to listen to NPR in the mornings, just like me. And he's a whiz at the piano. He serenaded me all night. And damn, what a voice! He's read so many of the same books that I have, and we stayed up talking until the sun came up both nights....

Make sure it works for you, dear one! This is meant to invoke emotion inside of your body.

You can listen to my audio on the book resources page at www.emyraldsinclaire.com/destinationsoulmate.

Repeat after me: I love myself, and I deserve to have everything my heart desires!

Day 3

Prayer Versus Meditation

"Religion is believing someone else's experience;
spirituality is having your own experience."

— Deepak Chopra

h, man. How many people did I just insult with that quote? Hopefully not you, and I hope you continue to read my book (we're almost there!). I have nothing against organized religion. I'm not religious myself. I've always thought of myself as spiritual instead.

And my spiritual practice involves meditation.

What is meditation? *(Oh Gawd, she's bringing up meditation again!)* It's giving yourself space in your mind away from the constant bombardment of thoughts.

I've always said that prayer is *asking* for what you want, while *meditation* is taking the time to listen for the answers. How can you truly hear the answers to your prayers and know what to do and where to go and who to see if you don't take time to listen?

And think of meditation as merely that. Shutting up so you can hear the answer to your heart's desires.

Today I'm sharing with you a guided meditation to exactly create what you want in this life.

 Exercise: Guided Meditation

Go to EmyraldSinclaire.com/destinationsoulmate and get yourself in a comfortable space and listen to the guided meditation.

Repeat after me: I love myself, and I deserve to have everything my heart desires!

Day 4

The Five Greatest

"Most people overestimate what they can
do in a year and they underestimate what
they can do in two or three decades."
—Tony Robbins

What are your five most significant accomplishments over the past 8 weeks?

Too often, we get caught up in everything we have NOT yet accomplished or everything left on our to-do list. Instead, I've been giving myself a new daily routine at the end of my day. I celebrate everything I accomplished for the day, instead of harping on everything that I didn't complete.

Instead of focusing on *lack*, I focus on how I'm *complete*.

Exercise: Your 5 Biggest Accomplishments

Pull out your journal and write down your five most significant accomplishments over the past 8 weeks.

When you've completed, give yourself a pat on the back (and perhaps a nice glass of wine).

As Esther Hicks always says: *The work is never over, and you're never complete.*

You are consistently a work in progress. But are you taking the time to keep score of where you started from and how much work and effort you've put in to get you to where you are today?

I remember the very first year of my love coaching business. I was sitting down to plan my next year's goals and dreams and got stuck with a big ol' case of *comparisonitis*. You see, I was disappointed that I wasn't at the six-figure mark. I was ashamed that I had racked up thousands of dollars of debt while creating my dream business. On and on this went for a while until a little voice inside of me said: *Emyrald, look at how far you've come in only a year!*

Then I started to make a list of everything I had accomplished in my first year of starting a business from scratch and accomplishments included: having 10 women in my group coaching program, growing my mailing list to 2,000 people, having a handful of private 1:1 clients with exceptional results and testimonials, building my website from scratch a number of times and perfecting my message.

And then I started to feel damn proud of myself. Like my man, Tony Robbins, who eloquently states that we overestimate what we can do within months but underestimate what we can do in a lifetime, I shifted my thinking around. It had only been a year for crying out loud! And it's only been (not even) 8 weeks for you! And look how far you've come.

I invite you to have big, freaking dreams, my dear. You still have the rest of your life ahead of you. Be patient. Enjoy the journey on the road to your dreams. And remember to take stock of where you are every once in a while and congratulate yourself for how far you've come!

Repeat after me: I love myself, and I deserve to have everything my heart desires!

$Day\ 5$

Never Look Back

"The only time you should ever look
back is to see how far you've come."
—Bangtan Boys, Butterfly

L et's continue to dig deeper into the reflection process of how
far you've come over the course of this book.

Exercise: Journal Questions

Pull out your journal and answer the following:

1. These are still my three most prominent limiting beliefs

2. These are my limiting beliefs flipped on their head, and now my new power mantras!

3. These are the most significant three aha moments I've had on this journey

You've come a long way. And you're not perfect. It's never over. You'll never be done. Today, all you have to do is take stock of the walls that still tower over you. Maybe they are huge. Maybe you already can feel a substantial energetic difference from when you began weeks ago. The point, however, is that you are here. You are putting one foot in front of the other. And you know what demons you are still up against.

But never look back out of remorse or regret. Everything in your journey brought you to where you are today.

And if you're like me and believe in reincarnation, well then, you probably wouldn't feel so much pressure to get it all perfect this go around.

Regardless of your belief system, give yourself another pat on the back because you've made some serious progress in the self-help department. And honestly, only YOU can help yourself.

Bravo.

Repeat after me: I love myself, and I deserve to have everything my heart desires!

Day 6

Ok, But How Do I
Really Change My Life?

"You'll never change your life until you change
something you do daily. The secret of your
success is found in your daily routine."

—John Maxwell

W e've gone over a shit-load in this book. And yes, I think
that is an actual measurement. And if we are talking
elephants…well dang!

And like Mr. Maxwell stated above, unless you change your daily
routines in your life, nothing is going to change. Even if you do the
exercises in this book, nothing will change unless you're creating a
habit of being a new person who thinks new thoughts who puts herself
in different situations.

You can think about being a new person, but now it's time to act
like this new person.

You've likely stuck with some of my suggestions and allowed other ones to fall to the way-side. And that's okay! I have my own personal routine every single day that changes based on what I'm reading or what is resonating for me at the moment.

Now it's time to build your new daily routine. Or to add to one you currently have by piecing together different things you've learned in this book.

Exercise: Refine Your Daily Routine

Flip through this book and your journal and make a list of all the various exercises and activities that you've done.

Go through that list and circle the ones that were the most powerful for you.

Next, write down a daily routine that you can do, including how many minutes for each exercise.

Then, STICK TO IT. Every. Single. Day.

And allow yourself to be open to new items coming into your life that resonate with the new you and allowing old habits and patterns to swiftly fall away when they no longer work for this new you that you're creating!

Repeat after me: I love myself, and I deserve to have everything my heart desires!

$\mathcal{D}ay\ 7$

Celebrate Good Times, Come On!

"Man cannot discover new oceans unless he has the courage to lose sight of the shore."

—Andre Gide

Woo! The last day of the last week. I'm so friggen proud of you! This truly is the time to celebrate your beautiful self and everything new you've learned.

 Exercise: 10 Tools

Pull out your lovely journal and answer the following prompt:

These are the 10 tools I'm going to use moving forward to keep the momentum going:

For example, hire a coach, find an accountability partner, continue with my gratitude journal, recite my affirmations every day...

And then, of course, you actually must use these 10 tools from here on out. You're a new person who is shooting rockets of new desires all over the place! And not only that, now you KNOW without a doubt that you can have everything your heart desires. You've just gotta practice a little faith and patience. And trust me, dear, I'm still working on the whole faith and trust and patience thing every single day.

And then.... you get to plan your celebration party! Your celebration party can be just you or you can invite your dearest friends.

What's a celebration party?

It's entirely up to you! What would make you super-duper happy right now? I'm a firm believer that we celebrate all of our hard work along the journey. And you just took a HUGE step towards the life that you crave.

A celebration party could involve buying yourself a new journal. Or it could mean flowers and dinner. Or your best friends come over, and you share with them your intention for life, love, and happiness.

But pull out your calendar right now and CELEBRATE YOURSELF within the next 7 days. You deserve a big ole celebration, so make sure you plan it!

Repeat after me: I love myself, and I deserve to have everything my heart desires!

The End

Happily Ever After... like for real? That stuff in the movies, does it really exist?

I have to be honest with you, and it hurts my heart to say it, so I'll say it real fast: *happilyeverafterdoesnotequalcupcakesandorgasmsallthetime.*

Whew. So, I said it.

Just because I've found my Personal Prince Charming - the love of my life - does not mean that the work ends there. And it certainly does not mean that life becomes a fairy tale. Yes, certain aspects are easier and that you're no longer single and crying into your wine glass each and every night. But when you find your spiritual match, you experience a whole different level of growth. So, on the one hand, sometimes things can actually get harder.

Happily Ever After is not for the weak; it's not for the faint of heart, and it's certainly not for those that are looking for someone to save them or fix them or complete them or take care of them. Happily Ever After is BEING a high-quality person ready for a mutually strong partner.

It's 100% give and 100% take. It's never 50/50. You accept radical responsibility for both the energy you are giving in a relationship and what you allow yourself to receive.

The road to Happily Ever After can be filled with twists and turns. You might get a flat and end up in a pothole. You might marry the love of your life…and then get divorced. You might be confronted by masked robbers or gremlins hiding under the bridge on your journey and lose it all.

Remember that song by Atlantis Morisette, *Ironic?*

"It's meeting the man of my dreams
And then meeting his beautiful wife
And isn't it ironic, don't you think?
A little too ironic, and yeah I really do think
It's like rain on your wedding day
It's a free ride when you've already paid
It's the good advice that you just didn't take
Who would've thought? It figures
Well, life has a funny way of sneaking up on you
And life has a funny way of helping you out
Helping you out."

The goal of finding Prince Charming and creating Happily Ever After involves finding a partner that will support you when life gets hard. It will be a reflection of the amount of support (and self love) that you are giving yourself. Yes, there will be challenging moments in life and *consciously doing the work* on yourself will ensure that you attract in a match that has done the same.

What you've learned in this book are tools to help you become a strong person focused upon spiritual and personal growth, and as a result, you will attract in a partner who also cares about evolving and growing as a human being.

I have absolute faith that no matter what life throws at you, you will be able to handle it, on your own and with your partner by your side.

You are stronger than you think. You are braver than you know. The power of creation flows through your veins.

You might walk through the fire. You might confront the dragon. But whatever it is that life has in store for you, you will come through it stronger, happier and more in love than ever before!

Now go out there and create your own Happily Ever After!

The End.

Xo,

Emyrald

P.S. The best way to *receive* love is to *give* love. So won't you please share the love and gift a copy of this book to a friend who could use it? The world needs more women in conscious and aligned partnerships and YOU can be part of that process! So spread the word of *Destination: Soulmate*, buy this book as a gift for your girlfriends, and be sure to share everything you've learned with those most important to you as a way to spread more love to the planet!

Remember, you get what you give so make sure to *give love*.

♥ THANK YOU!

They say it takes a village. So, thank you to everyone that helped support this book, but especially:

Jennifer - Thank you for the first round of editing you did for this book. I so appreciate your hard work and dedication.

Leah - Thank you for encouraging me to *finally* get the book published after sitting on it for years. Also, thanks for being my amazing bookkeeper and CPA from day 1. You were the best hire I ever made, and every day I count my lucky stars you're in my life.

My Friends, Family, and Past Clients - There are too many to name, but you know who you are! You all have been so supportive in my journey and I appreciate each and every one of you.

My Parents - I don't say it enough but I truly appreciate all the love, support and guidance you've provided over the years. Thank you for encouraging me to follow my heart and to be the best me I could possibly be!

You, Dear Reader - This book would not have been possible without you desiring the knowledge and doing the work to become a match for love. You've got this. I'm your biggest cheerleader and #1 Fan!

My Man - There are no words that can express how grateful I am for you, your support, and your love. So, until I can think of another word combination: Thank you. Thank you for being my lover, my partner and my very best friend. You're a source of constant inspiration and you inspire me to be a better woman each and every day. I'm truly grateful that I get to walk this path with you by my side. Falling in love (and being in love) with you was the easiest and most natural thing I've ever done.

Made in the USA
Monee, IL
25 February 2020